D0636968

001

EDINBURGH
the BEST!
THE ONE TRUE GUIDE

Peter Irvine
and
Keith Davidson

HarperCollins*Publishers*

HarperCollins Publishers
P.O. Box, Glasgow G4 0NB

First published 1998

Reprint 10 9 8 7 6 5 4 3 2 1 0

© Peter Irvine, 1998
Photographs: page 14 (© Malmaison), page 28 (© The Point), pages 30, 84 (© Keith Hunter), page 66 (© Valvona & Crolla), page 86 and section headings (© Stephen Whitehorne), page 124 (© Borthwick Castle)

Cover photograph: Central Edinburgh from Calton Hill (© Marius Alexander)

ISBN 0 00 472152 7

A catalogue record for this book is available from the British Library

Printed and bound in Great Britain by the Bath Press

CONTENTS

WHERE TO DRINK

WHERE TO GO IN TOWN

WHERE TO GO OUT OF TOWN

The telephone code for Edinburgh is 0131

INTRODUCTION

Welcome to the first edition of this city handbook extracted and updated from *Scotland the Best!* which, now in its fourth edition, has proven to be the most popular independent guide to our incredible country. Coming out every two years, it's the one the Scots use themselves, an insider guide written like this one by people who know and love their subject. Edinburgh is a big subject: here it has been reduced and condensed so that only the good information is included. You should need no other guide, but please let us know what you think – we thrive on feedback.

As you become familiar with *Edinburgh the Best!*, you will see that it is not quite like other guides. It doesn't give you lots of orientation information (it assumes you can negotiate your own arrival and can follow universal rules for survival in a new city) and you may need to consult a proper map (available free along with loads of other bumf from the Tourist Information Centres at the airport and near Waverley Station) since our maps are very diagrammatic. What it does give you in a broad range of categories is the best of what Edinburgh (and its immediate area) has to offer. We are highly selective and do not give all the options – only the best places. This includes the obvious, like the Castle, as well as the obscure, but nowhere is listed just because it's there – if it's mediocre, we ignore it. So, we're not too horrible about anyone – this is a positive book.

Although the selection process is undertaken by us, many people are consulted before choices are made and everywhere has been visited and sampled. We hope we are saving you the bother of having a less than satisfactory experience and we stand by all our recommendations. But nobody pays for inclusion, there are no ads, no subscriptions and no sponsorship. We do not employ a rigid set of standards and we tolerate idiosyncrasy because we'd rather have integrity and authenticity than mere amenity. Quality and attitude are what we recognize and want to bring to your attention. Service and atmosphere, attention to detail and value for money are all evaluated in making our decisions. This guide is written for you – not them – and not the 'industry'.

We want you to know that Edinburgh is one of the best cities on earth, and getting better all the time.

Enjoy it!

A DECLARATION OF FALLIBILITY

This guide is 'true', but it may not always be absolutely accurate. Since this may seem like a contradiction in terms, I should explain. *Edinburgh the Best!* is a handbook of information about all the 'best' places in Edinburgh. 'Best', you will understand, is a subjective term; it means 'best' according to what we think. Needless to say, there seem to be a lot of readers who agree with this judgement, and even if you don't you may see that I and my associates have gone to some efforts to reach our assertions. It's intended to be obvious that we are conveying opinions and impressions. They're true because the motives are true; we believe in what we are saying. We take no bribes and we have no vested interest in any of the places recommended, other than that we do talk things up and shamelessly proclaim the places we like or admire.

We hope it's plain where the facts end and the opinions begin. In guidebooks this is not always the case. However, it's with 'the facts' that inconsistencies may appear. We try to give accurate and clear directions explaining how to find a place and basic details that might be useful. This information is gleaned from a variety of sources and may be supplied by the establishment concerned. We do try to verify everything usually by visiting but things change and since nowhere we recommend has solicited their inclusion – we don't run copy past them – inaccuracies may occur. We hope that there aren't any, or many, but we may not find out until you let us know. We'd appreciate it if you would, so we can fix it for the next edition.

HOW TO USE THIS BOOK

There are three ways to use this book:

1. There's a straightforward index at the back. If you know somewhere already (and it's any good) you should find it here. Numbers refer to page numbers.

2. The book can be used by categories, e.g. you can look up the best French restaurants or the best pubs with outdoor drinking. Each entry has an item number in the outside margin. These are in numerical order and allow easy cross-referencing.

Categories are in groups, e.g. Where to Stay, Where to Eat. Each section has a map.

3. You can start with the maps and see how individual items are located, how they are grouped together, what's available in a particular area or what restaurants are recommended near where you are staying, for example.

The maps cover the city centre only and are not to scale. They are intended to be diagrammatic only. Each entry has a map reference which can be found beneath the item number in the border. If an item is out of the centre an arrow indicates its direction off the map. In the border this is denoted by an x, e.g. xD4 means 'Off the map at square D4'.

THE CELTIC CROSSES

Although everything listed in the book is notable and remarkable in some way, there are places that are outstanding even in this superlative company. Instead of marking them with a rosette or a star, they have been 'awarded' a Celtic cross symbol, the traditional Scottish version of the cross.

✝ Among the very best in Scotland

✝ ✝ Among the best (of its type) in the UK

✝ ✝ ✝ Among the best (of its type) in the world, or simply unique

A NOTE ON CATEGORIES

The book is arranged in five categories: Where to Stay; Where to Eat; Where to Drink; Where to Go (for general activities) in Town; and Where to Go out of Town. Within these five sections, categories range from the (mainly) very expensive, e.g. Best Hotels, to the fairly cheap, e.g. Best Hostels. The final section, Where to Go out of Town, lists places near to the city, easily reached by car or public transport and for a range of interests. Like most of the other items in *Edinburgh the Best!*, these have been extracted from *Scotland the Best!*, which covers the whole of the country.

THE CODES

1. The Item Code

At the outside margin of every item is a code which will enable you to find it on a map. Thus **152** *D3* should be read as follows: **152** is the item number, listed in a simple consecutive order; *D3* is the map coordinate, to help pinpoint the item's location on the map grid. A coordinate such as *xE1* indicates that the item can be reached by leaving the map at grid reference *E1*.

2. The Hotel Codes

Below each hotel recommended is a band of codes as follows:

20RMS   JAN-DEC   T/T   PETS   CC   KIDS   TOS   LOTS

20RMS   means the hotel has 20 bedrooms in total. No differentiation is made as to the type of room. Most hotels will offer twin rooms as singles or put extra beds in doubles if required. This code merely gives an impression of size.

JAN-DEC   means the hotel is open all year round. APR-OCT means approximately from the beginning of April to the end of October.

T/T   refers to the facilities: T/ means there are direct-dial phones in the bedrooms, while /T means there are TVs in the bedrooms.

PETS   means the hotel accepts dogs and other pets, probably under certain conditions (e.g. pets should be kept in the bedroom). It's usually best to check first.

XPETS   indicates that the hotel does not generally accept pets.

CC   means the hotel accepts major credit cards (e.g. Access, Visa).

XCC means the hotel does not accept major credit cards.

KIDS indicates children are welcome and special provisions/rates may be available.

XKIDS does not necessarily mean that children are not able to accompany their parents, only that special provisions/rates are not usually made. Check by phone.

TOS means the hotel is part of the Taste of Scotland scheme and has been selected for having a menu which features imaginative cooking using Scottish ingredients. The Taste of Scotland produces an annual guide of members.

LOTS Rooms which cost more than £60 per night per person. The theory is that if you can afford over £120 a room, it doesn't matter too much if it's £125 or £150. Other price bands are:

EXP Expensive: £50-60 per person.

MED.EXP Medium (expensive): £38-50.

MED.INX Medium (inexpensive): £28-38.

INX Inexpensive: £20-28.

CHP Cheap: less than £20.

Rates are per person per night. They are worked out by halving the published average rate for a twin room in high season and should be used only to give an impression of cost. They are based on 1997 prices. Add between £2 and £5 per year, though the band should stay the same unless the hotel undergoes improvements.

3. The Restaurant Code

Found at the bottom right of all restaurant entries. It refers to the price of an average dinner per person with a starter, a main course and a dessert. It doesn't include wine, coffee or extras.

EXP Expensive: more than £30.

MED Medium: £20-30.

INX Inexpensive: £12-20.

CHP Cheap: less than £12.

These are based on 1997 rates. With inflation, the relatige price bands should stay about the same.

4. The Walk Codes

A number of walks are described in the book. Below each walk is a band of codes as follows:

2-10km CIRC BIKE 1-A-1

2-10km means the walk(s) described may vary in length from 2km to 10km.

CIRC means the walk can be circular, while XCIRC shows the walk is not circular and you must return more or less by the way you came.

BIKE indicates the walk has a path which is suitable for ordinary bikes.

XBIKE means the walk is not suitable for, or does not permit, cycling.

MTBIKE means the track is suitable for mountain or all-terrain bikes.

The 1-A-1 Code

First number (1, 2, 3) indicates how easy the walk is.

1 the walk is easy; 2 medium difficulty, e.g. standard hillwalking, not dangerous nor requiring special knowledge or equipment; 3 difficult: care, preparation and a map are needed.

The letters (A, B, C) indicate how easy it is to find the path.

A the route is easy to find. The way is either marked or otherwise obvious; B the route is not very obvious, but you'll get there; C you will need a map and preparation or a guide.

The last number (1, 2, 3) indicates what to wear on your feet.

1 ordinary outdoor shoes, including trainers, are probably OK unless the ground is very wet; 2 you will need walking boots; 3 you will need serious walking or hiking boots.

Apart from the designated walks, the 1-A-1 code is employed wherever there is more than a short stroll required to get somewhere, e.g. a waterfall or a monument. The code appears at the bottom-right corner of the item.

LIST OF ABBREVIATIONS

As well as codes and because of obvious space limitations, a personal shorthand and ad hoc abbreviation system has had to be created. I'm the first to admit some may be annoying, especially 'restau' for restaurant, but it's a long word and it comes up often. The others which are used are:

accom	accommodation	incl	including
adj	adjacent	inexp	inexpensive
admn	admission	info	information
app	approach	jnct	junction
approx	approximately	L	loch
atmos	atmosphere	LO	last orders
av	average	min(s)	minute(s)
ave	avenue	N	north
AYR	all year round	no smk	no smoking
bedrms	bedrooms	nr	near
betw	between	NTS	National Trust for Scotland
br	bridge		
BYOB	bring your own bottle	o/look(s)	overlook(s)/ing
		opp	opposite
cl	closes/closed	o/side	outside
cres	crescent	pl	place
dining-rm	dining-room	poss	possible
dr	drive	pt	point/port
E	east	R	river
Edin	Edinburgh	r/bout	roundabout
esp	especially	rd	road
excl	excluding	refurb	refurbished/ment
exhib(s)	exhibition(s)	restau	restaurant
exp	expensive	rm(s)	room(s)
facs	facilities	rt	right
ft	fort	S	south
Glas	Glasgow	sq	square
gr	great	st	street
grd(s)	garden(s)	stn	station
hr(s)	hour(s)	SYHA	Scottish Youth Hostels Association
HS	Historic Scotland		

11

terr	terrace	v	very
TO	tourist information office	vac	vacation
t/off	turn-off	vegn	vegetarian
trad	traditional	W	west
tratt	trattoria	w/end(s)	weekend(s)
univ	university	yr(s)	year(s)

WHERE TO STAY

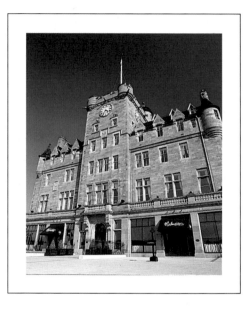

THE MALMAISON 'award-winning, praise-laden designer hotel' (page 18)

THE BEST HOTELS

✠ ✠ **THE BALMORAL:** 556 2414. Princes St at E end above Waverley Stn. Capital landmark with its clock always 2mins fast (except at Hogmanay) so you don't miss your train. The old pile changed hands again in spring 1997 and Sir Rocco Forte brought in the new broom, esp in the restau department. Exp for a mere tourist but if you can't afford to stay there's always afternoon tea in the Palm Court. Few hotels anywhere are so much in the heart of things. Good business centre, fine sports facs; luxurious and distinctive rms with some ethereal views of the city. Main restau, Number One Princes Street (61/BEST RESTAUS), and new brasserie, Hadrian's, both excellent.

1
D2

189RMS JAN-DEC T/T PETS CC KIDS LOTS

✠ ✠ **THE CALEDONIAN:** 459 9988. Princes St, W End. Edin institution – former stn hotel built in 1903. Owners have spent £8 million recently upgrading it from merely grand to Grand and Businesslike. Brand-new sports club opened in late summer 1997 (open to public), endearing lack of uniformity about the rms, executive rms on fifth floor have gr views as well as facs. Capital kind of place in every respect. Main restau, The Pompadour (62/BEST RESTAUS), is an experience.

2
C3

246RMS JAN-DEC T/T XPETS CC KIDS TOS LOTS

✠ ✠ **PRESTONFIELD HOUSE:** 668 3346. Off Priestfield Rd, 3km S of city centre. The Heilan' coos in the 14-acre grounds tell you this isn't your average urban bed for the night. 17th-century building with period features still intact. Architect Sir William Adam, responsible for the ceiling in the Tapestry Rm, also 'did' the ornamental ceilings in Holyrood Palace. Bulk of rms – 26 – added in a sympathetic 1997 refurb, though older ones possibly have more character. Enjoy the history wherever you sleep.

3
xE4

31RMS JAN-DEC T/T PETS CC XKIDS LOTS

✠ **CHANNINGS:** 315 2226. S Learmonth Gdns, parallel to Queensferry Rd after Dean Br. Diary of an Edwardian Urban Lady territory with 5 period town houses joined to form a v tasteful and discreet hotel. Impeccable décor with efficient and individual service. Gr views from top-floor rms, incl the Prime Minister's alma mater – Fettes College. A chic retreat from downtown throngs. Brasserie has sound reputation.

4
B2

48RMS JAN-DEC T/T XPETS CC KIDS LOTS

5
C1

✝ **THE HOWARD:** 557 3500. 36 Gt King St. Elegant establishment in the heart of the New Town – gr individual rms with cupboards big enough for a horse and some baths ditto. Basement restau, Number 36, is one of the city's finest (59/BEST RESTAUS) and a marked design contrast to what's upstairs. Same owners as Channings (*see above*).

15RMS JAN-DEC T/T XPETS CC XKIDS TOS LOTS

6
E2

ROYAL TERRACE: 557 3222. 18 Royal Terr. Romanesque plunge pool, other sports facs, multi-level terraced grd out back, deceptively large number of rms and town house décor a tad on the Baroque side. In other words, fabulous. Bar/restau not so notable among the natives, so good place for discreet meets.

94RMS JAN-DEC T/T XPETS CC KIDS LOTS

7
D3

HOLIDAY INN CROWN PLAZA: 557 9797. 80 High St. (Formerly the Scandic Crown.) Modern but sympathetic building on the Royal Mile, handy for everything. Good facs but some say service lacking. Thin walls, not gr views. Piano bar can be fun if taken in the right spirit. Gym and small pool. Unlike other hotels nr here, has parking.

238RMS JAN-DEC T/T PETS CC KIDS TOS LOTS

8
C3

THE SHERATON: 229 9131. Festival Sq on Lothian Rd and nr Conference Centre, this city-centre business hotel won no prizes for architecture when it opened late 1980s, but further refurbs have tartaned it up and brought some cosiness to the concrete. A reliable stopover with excellent service. Larger rms and castle views carry premiums, but make big difference. Terrace restau adequate, but The Grill menu prepared under the supervision of Nicolas Laurent is elegant, Scottish and innovative.

261RMS JAN-DEC T/T PETS CC KIDS TOS LOTS

9
C2

THE GEORGE: 225 1251. George St (betw Hanover St and St Andrew Sq). An Inter-Continental Hotel but Robert Adam-designed and dating back to late 18th century. Good views to Fife from the top 2 floors. Pricey, but you pay for the location and the Georgian niceties. Busy and grandiose carvery plus good Gallic restau, the Chambertin (87/FRENCH RESTAUS).

195RMS JAN-DEC T/T PETS CC KIDS LOTS

Holyrood Palace

Holyrood Park

Calton Hill

QUEENS DRIVE

THE PLEASANCE

LONDON ROAD

LEITH WALK

NICOLSON STREET

CLARK STREET

BROUGHTON ST.

YORK PLACE

LEITH ST.

NORTH BRIDGE

SOUTH BRIDGE

BLAIR ST.

University

Museum

COCKBURN ST.

Waverley Station

MARKET ST.

WAVERLEY BRIDGE

GEORGE IV BRIDGE

CANDLEMAKER ROW

GRASSMARKET

LAURISTON PLACE

Princes Street Gardens

The Meadows

MELVILLE DRIVE

Castle

WEST PORT

THE MOUND

HANOVER STREET

FREDERICK STREET

CASTLE STREET

CHARLOTTE SQ.

P R I N C E S   S T R E E T

G E O R G E   S T R E E T

QUEEN STREET

GREAT KING STREET

DUNDAS STREET

HOWE STREET

ST VINCENT ST.

HERIOT ROW

INDIA STREET

GLOUCESTER LANE

DUBLIN STREET

DUNDAS STREET

HENDERSON ROW

RABURN PLACE

Stockbridge

GLENOGLE ROAD

NW CIRCUS PLACE

INDIA PLACE

COMELY BANK AVENUE

QUEENSFERRY

QUEENSFERRY ROAD

LOTHIAN ROAD

MORRISON STREET

HAYMARKET TERRACE

Haymarket Station

DALRY ROAD

BREAD STREET

LEVEN STREET

HOME STREET

TOLLCROSS

3

6

7

5

9

4

8

THE MORE INDIVIDUAL HOTELS

10
xE1

✠ ✠ **THE MALMAISON:** 555 6868. Tower Pl, Leith, at the dock gates. Award-winning, praise-laden designer hotel with individual and rather natty rms. *Wired* magazine called it 'rock 'n' roll'. Raging success; more than doubled its accom in autumn 1997. CD players in each *chambre* (borrow CDs from reception). Brasserie and café-bar have stylish ambience too (72/BEST BISTROS) and there are many others nearby in this waterfront quarter. Also in Glas and spreading S as we speak.

60RMS JAN-DEC T/T PETS CC KIDS EXP

11
C3

✠ **THE POINT:** 221 9919. 34 Bread St. You'd never guess this used to be a Co-operative department store. Space and colour combinations manage to look simultaneously rich and minimal, some castle views. Suites (LOTS) come with side-lit Jacuzzis. You'll feel more like a film extra than a hotel guest in this rather handsome bed boutique. New café-bar Monboddo and restau have modern and spacious, mid-Euro feel. Good places to meet Edinburgers.

95RMS JAN-DEC T/T PETS CC KIDS EXP

12
C2

26 NORTHUMBERLAND ST: 556 1078. Jim and Aurore Sibbet have retired and are now in partnership with Jens and Anita Steffen so under new management, but not new ownership. Still the same remarkable Georgian town house that has been wowing guests for yrs. Timeless.

5RMS JAN-DEC T/T XPETS CC KIDS MED.EXP

13
C2

17 ABERCROMBY PLACE: 557 8036. Another plush and private Georgian town house; discreet lack of signage. Once abode of the New Town's architect, Playfair, now belongs to advocate Eirlys Lloyd. No smk, 2 rms in a self-contained mews; main house for breakfast.

8RMS JAN-DEC T/T XPETS CC KIDS MED.EXP

14
D2

THE ALBANY: 556 0397. 39 Albany St. Completely changed hotel due to new owners and total refurb spring 1997. Not cheap, but now featuring that New Town splendour and *politesse* – only a few mins walk uphill to Princes St. Basement restau, Haldane's (135/SCOTTISH RESTAUS), is pretty good.

21RMS JAN-DEC T/T PETS CC KIDS LOTS

15
D3

BANK HOTEL: 556 9043. Corner of S Br and Royal Mile. Former bank converted into café-bar with bedrms above, most with urban views. Rm service minimal and not all en-suite. Like bar downstairs (the Logie Baird) all have Scottish theme – stretching the tartan too far? 9RMS JAN-DEC T/T XPETS CC KIDS MED.EXP

SIX ST MARY'S PLACE: 332 8965. On main st of Stockbridge (St Mary's Pl part of Raeburn Pl) and busy main rd out of town for Forth Rd Br and N, this is a tastefully converted Georgian town house. Informal, friendly, well-cared-for accom popular with academics and people we like. No smk. Vegn. Breakfast in conservatory. Jolly nice people.

16
B1

8RMS JAN-DEC X/X XPETS CC KIDS MED.INX

STUART HOUSE: 557 9030. 12 E Claremont St. Nr the corner of main rd and pleasant walk up to Princes St (1.5km). Residential New Town st and family house decorated with taste and attention to detail – bonny flower grd out front. Book well in advance. No smk. 7RMS JAN-DEC T/T XPETS CC KIDS MED.EXP

17
D1

2 BONNINGTON TERRACE: 554 9007. Just by jnct of Ferry Rd and Newhaven Rd. Gillie McCowan Hill's tastefully furnished and welcoming house is the sort of place *StheB!* researchers would stay. No B&B sign at gate and do not confuse with guesthouse next door. Understated interior design qualities so good they make you want to spit. 3RMS JAN-DEC X/T PETS CC KIDS MED.INX

18
xE1

TEVIOTDALE HOUSE: 667 4376. 53 Grange Loan, towards E end. Fabulous fecund flower grd out front and bargain accom within. Ground-floor rm (popular with honeymooners) has a 4-poster with adj chaise longue and the whole effect is undeniably, unexpectedly sexy – although v respectable you understand. Healthy breakfasts. 7RMS JAN-DEC T/T XPETS CC KIDS MED.INX

19
xD4

HOTEL JAVA: 467 7527. Constitution St, Leith next to the estimable Port O' Leith (239/GREAT EDIN PUBS). Friendly, contemporary bar with basic but inexp rms in Leith nr docks and with many of the city's best bars and restaus nearby. Phillipa and Sue run a laid-back and happy house. Rms at back and round courtyard.

20
xE1

10RMS JAN-DEC X/X PETS CC KIDS CHP

WEST END HOTEL: 225 3656. 35 Palmerston Pl. Capital haunt for Highlanders and Islanders who feel like a blether in Gaelic or a good folk music session in the bar (decent measures). Popular with folkie non-guests too. Spacious rms with oddly familiar furniture.

21
B3

8RMS JAN-DEC T/T XPETS CC KIDS INX

THE BEST 'ECONOMY' HOTELS AND TRAVEL-LODGES

Hotels/B&Bs below are included on grounds of price, convenience or just because we like them for some idiosyncratic reason.

22
C3

THE APEX: 300 3456. 31-35 Grassmarket. Once part of Heriot-Watt Univ, a determined conversion resulted in a central hotel with contemporary Euro-bland façade. Civilised although a tad characterless, main market is business but flat rate charge per rm attracts families and the occasional hen night (4 lassies in a rm equals CHP). Extra charge for rms with castle view, fifth-floor restau (INX) also has nice outlook. Another Apex (474 3456) opened nr Haymarket Stn late 1997 with 68 rms and a restau called Tabu which has received mixed reviews.

99RMS   JAN-DEC   T/T   XPETS   CC   KIDS   MED.EXP

23
E2

PARLIAMENT HOUSE: 478 4000. 15 Calton Hill. Good central location, only 200m from E end of Princes St and adj to Calton Hill (347/BEST VIEWS). New on the scene, opened autumn 1996. Decidedly minimalist in terms of service – no restau or bar and Continental breakfast taken in your rm – but smart town housestyle décor.

54RMS   JAN-DEC   T/T   XPETS   CC   KIDS   MED.EXP

24
D3

STATION HOTEL: 226 1446. 9-13 Market St, behind Waverley Stn. Some good views from upper floors to Princes St. Couldn't be handier for the stn or city centre. Rms feel a bit 'holiday package deal', basic but acceptable. No smk. Its restau is Italian-ish and curiously always empty.

30RMS   JAN-DEC   T/T   XPETS   CC   KIDS   MED.EXP

25
xA3

STAKIS EDINBURGH AIRPORT: 519 4400. At the airport, 10km W of city centre. No way 'economy', but a reliable travellers' tryst. An L-shaped box with the buzz of a high-class transit camp; charming staff. You can virtually roll out of bed and check in.

134RMS   JAN-DEC   T/T   XPETS   CC   KIDS   LOTS

26
B3

TRAVEL INN: 228 9819. 1 Morrison Link, nr Haymarket Stn. Likeable for the fact it makes no pretence to be anything other than a bed factory. Big, orthogonal and dull but v cheap – flat charge of under £40 applies per rm which can take 2 adults or a family of 4. 7 rms specially adapted for wheelchair users. Expanding to truly monster size in 1998.

128RMS   JAN-DEC   X/T   XPETS   CC   KIDS   CHP

FORTE POSTHOUSE: 334 0390. Corstorphine Rd next to Zoo. Entrance feels like an underground car park, but there's a gr view across to the Pentlands. Bit of a featureless bed box all told, but has all the facs expected of a big chain hotel and you get to listen to Cheetah and his chums at night.

204RMS   JAN-DEC   T/T   PETS   CC   KIDS   MED.EXP

THISTLE INN: 220 2299. 94-96 Grassmarket. Taken over in summer 1997 by a major brewery so changes poss. Otherwise, basic and boisterously located accom joined to Biddy Mulligan's (309/IRISH BARS) next door which is open to 1am, 7 days. So don't bring grandma, do come on a night out with the lads (or lassies).

29RMS   JAN-DEC   X/T   PETS   CC   KIDS   MED.INX

IBIS: 240 7000. Hunter Sq. Just opened at time of going to press, so no cross-referencing number, I'm afraid. First in Scotland of the Euro budget chain and first in Edin of a huge rash of new hotels. Dead central behind the Tron so good for Hogmanay stays (or not). Serviceable and efficient. For tourists, poss the best of the ones above for location.

97RMS   JAN-DEC   T/T   PETS   CC   KIDS   MED.INX

THE BEST HOSTELS

Edin has some YHA hostels (nae drinking) and independents (young and Hoochy, open 24hrs), also some handy univ halls of residence to let o/side term time. With all the independent hostels, it's best to turn up around 11/11.30am if you haven't booked. The SYHA is the Scottish Youth Hostels Association. 01786 891400 for details, or contact any YHA hostel. Bus information: 225 3858.

29
D3

♰ ♰ **THE HIGH STREET HOSTEL:** 557 3984. 8 Blackfriars St. Out the door, turn left and you're on the Royal Mile, turn rt for the Cowgate with its late-night bars. Ideal central cheap 24hr crash-out dormitory accom with all the facs for itinerant youth seeking a capital experience. Two sister hostels: **ROYAL MILE BACK-PACKERS**, 105 High St (557 6120); **CASTLE ROCK**, 15 Johnston Terr (225 9666) are both in the same area. Castle Rock, in the old Council Environmental Health HQ, is huge (150 beds in various dorms, but no singles/doubles) and has some gr views across the Grassmarket or to the castle which is just over there. Same folk (Mr Backpacker himself, Peter Macmillan) also have places in Ft William, Inverness, Oban and Skye. CHP

Late news at time of going to press: High St Hostel may close soon due to expansion of Holiday Inn next door. We say shame, this is one of Scotland's pioneer new-style hostels.

30
A3

♰ ♰ **S.Y. HOSTEL, EGLINTON:** 337 1120. 18 Eglinton Cres. From the stained glass over the main door to the tartan and wood entrance foyer, you know you're not in a typical hostel. Grand late-Victorian pile in a quiet W End st with 144 beds – majority in dorms but some rms for 4. Members only but you can join at reception. Booking recommended. Cl for a month in winter. Doors locked at 2am. CHP

31
A2

♰ **BELFORD HOSTEL:** 225 6209. Douglas Grds, nr National Gallery of Modern Art (excellent café, 180/BEST TEAROOMS) and quaint Dean Village, but still fairly central. Bizarre concept – 110 beds in partitioned-off 'rms' of 6-10 in a converted church. Top-bunk berth gets you a view of the vaulted wooden ceiling way above. Games rm, bar, MTV. Sister establishment is **EDINBURGH BACKPACKERS HOSTEL**, 65 Cockburn St (220 1717). CHP

32
D2

PRINCES ST HOSTEL: 556 6894. 5 W Register St. Behind Burger King at E end of Princes St. Incredibly central for cheap accom. Basic and attracts the usual international crowd. Same people now have **PRINCES ST WEST**, 3 Queensferry St (226 2939) with bar. CHP

S.Y. HOSTEL, BRUNTSFIELD: 447 2994. 7 Bruntsfield Cres. S of Tollcross about 10mins walk from W End. Buses from Princes St (grd side), nos 11, 15, 16. Reliable and secure hostel accom in a verdant corner of Bruntsfield. 158 beds but booking 2-3 months in advance is essential at peak times. Again, members only, join at reception and doors locked at 2am. CHP

33
xD4

From July-Sep, SYHA also opens a temporary hostel in **ROBERTSON'S CLOSE** off Cowgate. Phone Edin district office for info 229 8660.

POLLOCK HALLS: 667 0662. Off Dalkeith Rd. The main accom for Edin Univ – a village of modern low-rise blocks, situated 3km S of centre next to the Royal Commonwealth Swimming Pool (334/MAIN ATTRACTIONS) and in the shadow of Arthur's Seat, on which to gaze or jog. Refectory, bar, shared kitchens and showers. Huge number of rms – 800 basic singles and more than 400 others, some doubles. Vacs only. MED.INX

34
xE4

NAPIER UNIVERSITY: 455 4291. Craiglockhart campus off Colinton Rd. College halls in high-rise blocks about 10km SW of centre. In grounds of imposing Craiglockhart Hospital where Siegfried Sassoon met Wilfred Owen. Too far out for some, but buses nos 23 and 27 from the Mound (Princes St). V good sports facs, incl pool. Full meal service sometimes poss. Vacs only, availability may depend on conferences. B&B. Good value. CHP

35
xC4

Higher education expansion means Napier now has a fair number of student flats to let during vacs for 4, 5 or 6 people – weekly rate (CHP). 455 4211 for info.

QUEEN MARGARET COLLEGE: 317 3310. Clerwood Terr. Way out, midway betw main rds W to Glas and N to Forth Br; about 10km, so transport probably essential (or bus). Campus facs, e.g. refectory, laundry, bank, good sports. Shared bathrms, etc. and a bit dreary, so not exceptional value, but a private and well-equipped refuge from uptown hassles. Phone first. Also self-catering flats. Vacs only. CHP

36
xA2

THE BEST CAMPING AND CARAVAN PARKS

Refer to Lothians map on pages 116–17.

37
C2

MORTONHALL PARK: 664 1533. Off Frogston Rd E, a kind of inner-city ring rd. About 12km S of centre. From S and city bypass: take Lothianburn jnct into town and rt at first lights for 4km. From centre: take A702 via Morningside to last left turn before bypass. Mortonhall marked, but enter via (and pass) Klondyke Grd Centre. No. 7 or 11 bus from town. Well-equipped park with 4 toilet/shower blocks, shop, laundry, lounge, play area and fully serviced pitches. Also bar/restau in converted stables/courtyard serving food until 9pm. Coffee shop with decent home-baking at grd centre. Mar-Oct. 268 places.

38
C1

THE EDINBURGH CARAVAN CLUB SITE: 312 6874. Marine Dr, Silverknowes. 8km NW of centre via Ferry Rd then rt on Pennywell Rd, continue over r/bout to Marine Dr. Former local authority site, taken over and substantially refurb by the Caravan Club of GB – reopened Aug 1997. Accepts non-members. 200 pitches for caravans, tents and motor homes – all with electricity. Two heated toilet blocks, laundry, disabled facs. Open AYR.

39
C2

FORDEL, DALKEITH: 660 3921. Lauder Rd. On A68, 4km S of Dalkeith; 18km SE of centre. V well equipped and serviced site secluded from the busy rd. Behind a 24hr garage and pub/café (Fordel Inn). Some work done recently so improved pitches and more landscaping. Best to have a car; reasonable bus service to Dalkeith, but fewer go past gate. 110 pitches.

40
C1

DRUM MOHR, MUSSELBURGH: 665 6867. Levenhall. 4km out of Musselburgh on the coast rd to Prestonpans. 22km E of centre. Go through Musselburgh, signed off bypass and take rd rt at Mining Museum. Award-winning site is 400m up a country lane, within sight of the sea, quiet (apart from some traffic noise) and well maintained. You will be rather removed from Edin, but within easy reach of the golf/beaches/walks and ice cream of E Lothian. Disabled facs. Mar-Oct. 120 pitches.

41
D1

GOSFORD GARDENS, ABERLADY: 01875 870487. Off the A198, the coast rd off the A1 35km E of Edin. Caravan Club of GB site in former walled grd nr Aberlady. Attractive, secluded but perhaps too intimate for some. 120 pitches. No tents.

THE BEST HOTELS
OUTSIDE TOWN

See Lothians map on pages 116–17.

✠ ✠ **GREYWALLS, GULLANE:** 01620 842144. On the coast, 36km E of Edin off A198 just beyond golfers' paradise of Gullane. O/looks Muirfield, the championship course (no right of access) and nr Gullane's 3 courses and N Berwick's 2 (361/362/SPORTS FACILITIES). No grey walls here but warm sandstone and light, summery public rms in this Lutyens-designed manor with grds attributed to Gertrude Jekyll. It's the look that makes it special and the roses are legendary. Sculpture grd in July and literary w/ends. Library like a London club, and service. Golf ain't everything. 22RMS APR-OCT T/T PETS CC XKIDS TOS LOTS

42
D1

✠ **BORTHWICK CASTLE, NORTH MIDDLETON:** 01875 820514. On B6367, 3km off the A7, 18km bypass, 26km SE of centre. Accept no substitute – if you want to stay in a real Border castle go for the big red one. Walls 30m high, this magnificent tower house knocks you off your horse with its authenticity – Mary Queen of Scots was blockaded here once and at night you expect to see her swishing up the spiral stairs. 8 rms in castle, 2 in gatehouse, the (v) grand banqueting hall is impressive, dinner (EXP) is not. 10RMS MAR-DEC T/X PETS CC KIDS TOS LOTS

43
C2

✠ **JOHNSTOUNBURN HOUSE, HUMBIE:** 01875 833696. On B6457 2km from A68 and 25km SE of centre. Bypass 22km. Country class in this 17th-century manor with relaxed and friendly service. Some rms in its coach house, all have that upbeat frilliness. Public areas v cool, esp the panelled 18th-century dining-rm. Feels like a true escape. Mavis Hall park adj offers clay pigeon shooting, fishing, off-road, etc, so it's an excellent all-round centre v close to the city. Cream of the county. 19RMS JAN-DEC T/T PETS CC KIDS TOS LOTS

44
C2

✠ **NORTON HOUSE, INGLISTON:** 333 1275. Off A8 nr airport, 10km W of city centre. Virgin hotel in extensive grounds (hence quiet) with those Bransonesque touches you'll love or loathe – teddy bear on the bed, ducks in the bath. But high standard of service and accom with country house feel and handy for the expanding business theme parks nearby. Conservatory Restau is easily worth its two AA rosettes. 47RMS JAN-DEC T/T XPETS CC KIDS TOS LOTS

45
B1

46
C2

DALHOUSIE CASTLE, BONNYRIGG: 01875 820153. Just off B704 2km from the A7, 15km from bypass and 23km S of centre. The castle that tries too hard? It looks fantastic in its setting and dates way back to the 13th century but the facs are everything you would expect from a contemporary city hotel, which is perversely disappointing. (Previous guests incl Edward I, Cromwell, Queen Victoria and assorted rock stars.) Our Braveheart researcher was quite fond of the William Wallace rm; dinner is taken in the dungeon. Another 5 rms in adj Victorian lodge.

29RMS JAN-DEC T/T PETS CC KIDS TOS LOTS

47
B1

HOUSTON HOUSE, UPHALL: 01506 853831. On A899 at end of Broxburn/Uphall Main St, 8km from r/bout at the start of the M8 Edin–Glas motorway. Airport 10km, 18km W of centre. Bits of this tower house date to the 16th century, others far more recent (extension with 46 rms completed summer 1997). Yet more 4-posters, nice open fire in the bar, restau is rated and the place is stuffed with farmers during Royal Highland Show week. Set on 20 acres of greenery, atypical Uphall. New sports facs, incl a pool.

72RMS JAN-DEC T/T XPETS CC KIDS TOS LOTS

48
B2

DALMAHOY, KIRKNEWTON: 333 1845. On A71 (Kilmarnock rd) on edge of town – bypass 5km, 15km W of centre, airport 6km. In the beginning was the word, and the word was golf. 2 good courses, European Tour venue and that's what the groups of chaps (and occasionally ladies) come for. Hotel itself is Georgian with 7 distinctive rms, rest in new annexe where the extensive sports facs reside. Part of the Marriott chain.

151RMS JAN-DEC T/T XPETS CC KIDS TOS LOTS

49
D1

MARINE HOTEL, NORTH BERWICK: 01620 892406. The grand old seaside hotel of N Berwick reeks of holidays gone by – you almost expect to see Margaret Rutherford on the putting green. Snooker, open-air swimming pool. O/looks links and Fidra. Good for kids and golf. 83RMS JAN-DEC T/T PETS CC KIDS EXP

50
D1

OPEN ARMS, DIRLETON: 01620 850241. Dirleton is 4km from Gullane towards N Berwick. Comfortable if pricey hotel in centre of village, opp ruins of castle. Location means it's a golfers' paradise and special packages are available. Restau has 2 AA whatsits.

10RMS JAN-DEC T/T PETS CC KIDS TOS LOTS

HAWES INN, SOUTH QUEENSFERRY: 331 1990. From city take rd N via Queensferry Rd heading for Forth Rd Br. On front at Hawes Pier and literally under the famous rail br (335/MAIN ATTRACTIONS). Pick the rt rm and lie back in the 4-poster to soak up an atmos that made RLS escape into the fantasy world of *Kidnapped*. Facs far from fab, but genuine 16th century with unique situation.

8RMS (NONE *EN SUITE*)   JAN-DEC   T/T   PETS   CC   KIDS   MED.INX

QUEENSFERRY LODGE HOTEL, nr NORTH QUEENSFERRY: 01383 410000. At Fife end of rd br (so Edin is a toll away), but a good stopping-off place for all points N. Dramatic setting with estuarine views. Restaus/bars/shop – a modern purpose-built roadhouse. N Queensferry less crowded than S (except for Deep Sea World – 446/WHERE TO TAKE KIDS); nice bistro – the Channel (01383 412567).

32RMS   JAN-DEC   T/T   PETS   CC   KIDS   MED.INX

THE OLD ABERLADY INN: 01875 870503. Main St. Straightforward drop inn with simple, well-kept rms, a good farmhouse-style bistro with interesting menu and a trad howff for drinks and bar food. Popular with golfers – OK for anyone.

8RMS   JAN-DEC   T/T   PETS   CC   KIDS   MED.INX

TWEEDDALE ARMS, GIFFORD: 01620 810240. One of 2 inns in this heart of E Lothian village 9km from the A1 at Haddington, within easy reach of Edin. Set among rich farming country, Gifford is conservative and couthy. Some bedrms small, but public rms v pleasant. Smells like a country inn should.

16RMS   JAN-DEC   T/T   PETS   CC   KIDS   MED.INX

51
B1

52
B1

53
D1

54
D2

THE POINT 'you'll feel more like a film extra than a hotel guest' (page 18)

WHERE TO EAT

INDIGO YARD 'enormously popular and always buzzing' (page 34)

THE BEST RESTAURANTS

✝ ✝ **THE ATRIUM:** 228 8882. Foyer of the Traverse Theatre (387/GOOD NIGHTLIFE), Cambridge St off Lothian Rd. Naked flames, strangely-lit chefs visible in the open kitchen, intelligent service, striking design and that wonderful 'wine reduction' smell. Add some quite remarkable food that's both modish and subtle and you have the capital's best all-rounder – courtesy of Andrew Radford. The newer **BLUE** (66/BEST BISTROS)is upstairs. Lunch and dinner Mon-Sat. LO 10pm. Cl Sun. EXP

55
C3

✝ ✝ **LA POTINIÈRE:** Main St, Gullane. 01620 843214. 36km W of city on A198 coast rd off A1. David and Hilary Brown's intimate, much celebrated caff, the first truly gr restau in SE Scotland and still up there though facing stiffer competition in town. Worth the 45min drive for the elegant simplicity of their set menu of French classic and contemporary *gastronomie*. Outstanding wine list. Dinner: Fri/Sat only (or groups by arrangement). Lunch: (Tue-Sun). Famously booked in advance, but lunch and Fri easier and often cancellations. No smk. MED

56
xE2

✝ **THE WITCHERY:** 225 5613. Castlehill. At the top of the Royal Mile where the tourists throng, but many will be unaware that this is one of the city's best restaus and certainly its most stylishly atmospheric. 2 salons, the upper more witchery; in the 'secret grd' downstairs, a converted school playground, James Thompson has created a more spacious ambience for the (same) elegant Scottish menu. 7 days. Lunch and dinner. (214/LATE-NIGHT RESTAUS) EXP

57
C3

✝ **(fitz)HENRY:** 555 6625. 19 Shore Pl. The inimitable Dave Ramsden has worked hard to turn his warehouse brasserie in an off-the-waterfront st in Leith into one of Edin's top spots, the only one (1997) apart from the Atrium to get a Michelin red M. Chef Herve Veraille is the other reason. Fastidious, but non-intrusive service in a stylish setting. 6 days. Lunch and dinner. Cl Sun. MED

58
xE1

✝ **NUMBER 36:** 556 3636. Basement restau of the Howard Hotel (5/BEST HOTELS) in the New Town and in design contrast to the Georgian opulence upstairs. Number 36 is bold and clean-cut verging on minimalist. The food also is contemporary in every respect and when it opened in 1997, 36 quickly became one of *the* places to eat. Malcolm Warham is the chef heading, I suspect, for accolades other than this. 7 days. Lunch and dinner (cl Sat lunch). No smk. MED

59
C1

60
xE1

✚ **THE VINTNER'S ROOM:** 554 6767. 87 Giles St, Leith. Cobbled courtyard to wine bar, with woody ambience and open fire. Vaults, formerly used to store claret (Leith was an important wine pt), also incl a restaurant lit by candlelight. Bar and restau have same evening menu (French tone using fresh Scottish produce), but cheaper options at lunch in the bar and less formal. Excellent cheeseboard and wine list. Mon-Sat lunch and 6.30-10pm.   MED

61
D2

✚ **NUMBER ONE PRINCES STREET, BALMORAL HOTEL:** 556 2414. Address with a certain ring for the principal restau of the Balmoral (1/BEST HOTELS) entered through lobby or off st. Based apparently on the Mandarin Grill, Hong Kong, these opulent subterranean salons have ample space around the tables, but the lighting and lacquering do little to cosify the ritziness. Chef Jeff Bland, ensures that the revamped **HADRIAN'S BRASSERIE** at st level complements well. Cl Sat/Sun lunch. LO 10.30pm.   EXP

62
C3

✚ **THE POMPADOUR, CALEDONIAN HOTEL:** 459 9988. Princes St. One of the most exp meals in town but a sensual assault on several levels: a pianist plays, waiters glide, the salon is ornate and the food – French style by Jerome Barbançon – careers between hauntingly simple to pure mental intricate (chocolate pud in the shape of a grand piano). It could intimidate the socks off some of us, but no worries – manager Jordi Figuerola will see you rt. Dinner only, Tue-Sat. LO 10pm. (2/BEST HOTELS)   EXP

63
C2

✚ **MARTIN'S:** 225 3106. 70 Rose St N Lane. Shabby lane behind busy shopping precinct nr Princes St – odd place to find a top restau but Martin probably likes it that way. Good service, v high standard of contemporary cooking, delicate desserts and an unsurpassed, unpasteurised Celtic cheeseboard. He knows his wines. Lunch Tue-Fri, dinner Tue-Sat. LO 10pm.   EXP

64
xE1

THE ROCK: 555 2225. Commercial St/Quay, Leith. In a row of 'waterfront' restaus in converted warehouses opp the new Scottish Office, this is the one that stands out for excellent food (though others are notable). Modern setup with good sightlines to other diners and open kitchen. Grill menu of burgers and steaks (and salmon) is simple and à la carte menu widens choice for non redmeaters. Gr chips. Easy place to drop in but you do dine. 7 days. Lunch and dinner. Cl Sat lunch, Sun dinner.   MED

65
xE1

WINTER GLEN: 477 7060. 3a1 Dundas St. Report: 131/SCOTTISH.

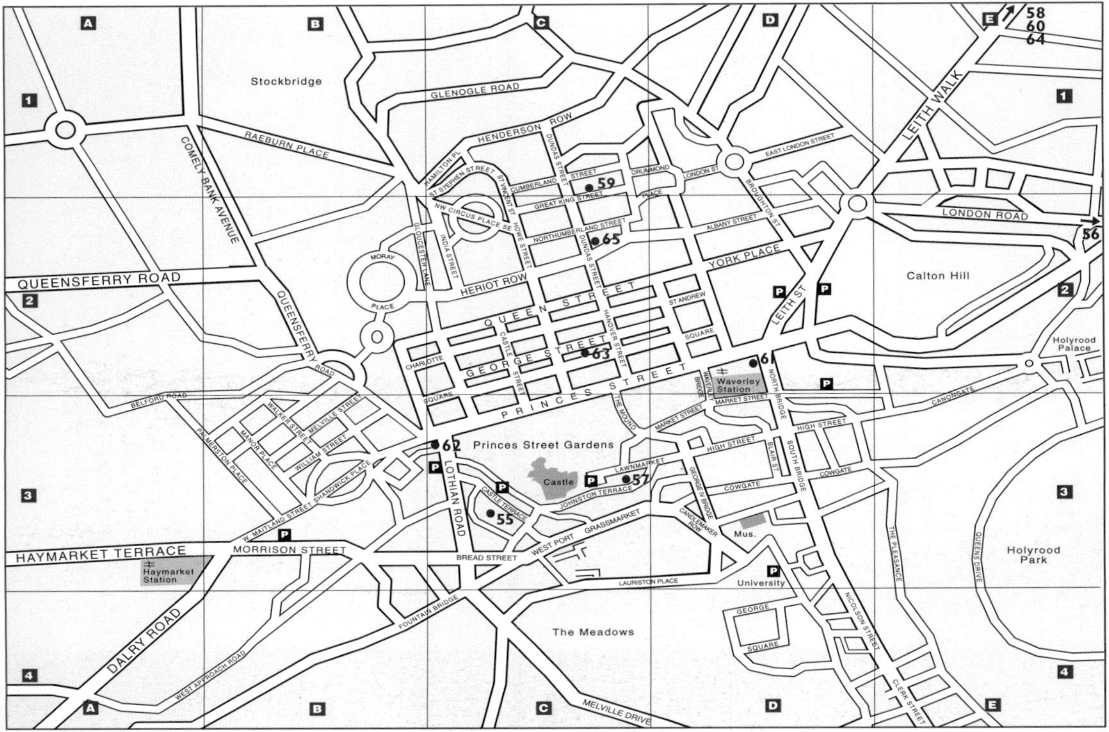
58
60
64
56
Stockbridge
Calton Hill
Holyrood Palace
Holyrood Park
The Meadows
Princes Street Gardens
Castle
Mus.
University
Waverley Station
Haymarket Station
GLENOGLE ROAD
RAEBURN PLACE
COMELY BANK AVENUE
QUEENSFERRY ROAD
QUEENSFERRY ROAD
HENDERSON ROW
HAMILTON PL
ST STEPHEN STREET
ST VINCENT ST
CUMBERLAND STREET
DUNDAS STREET
DRUMMOND PLACE
LONDON ST
EAST LONDON STREET
LEITH WALK
LONDON ROAD
BROUGHTON ST
ALBANY STREET
GREAT KING STREET
NORTHUMBERLAND STREET
NW CIRCUS PLACE SE
HOWE STREET
INDIA STREET
GLOUCESTER LANE
MORAY PLACE
HERIOT ROW
YORK PLACE
QUEEN STREET
ST ANDREW SQUARE
LEITH ST
CASTLE STREET
HANOVER STREET
CHARLOTTE SQUARE
GEORGE STREET
PRINCES STREET
BELFORD ROAD
WALKER STREET
MELVILLE STREET
MANOR PLACE
WILLIAM STREET
PALMERSTON PLACE
SHANDWICK PLACE
W. MAITLAND STREET
THE MOUND
WAVERLEY BRIDGE
MARKET STREET
NORTH BRIDGE
CANONGATE
HIGH STREET
BLAIR ST
SOUTH BRIDGE
COWGATE
LAWNMARKET
JOHNSTON TERRACE
CASTLE TERRACE
LOTHIAN ROAD
GRASSMARKET
GEORGE IV BRIDGE
CANDLEMAKER ROW
WEST PORT
BREAD STREET
HAYMARKET TERRACE
MORRISON STREET
LAURISTON PLACE
FOUNTAIN BRIDGE
DALRY ROAD
WEST APPROACH ROAD
MELVILLE DRIVE
GEORGE SQUARE
NICOLSON STREET
CLERK STREET
THE PLEASANCE
QUEENS DRIVE
59
65
63
61
62
57
55

THE BEST BISTROS AND CAFÉ-BARS

All open for lunch unless otherwise stated.

66
C3

✝ ✝ **BLUE:** 221 1222. Cambridge St. Upstairs in the Traverse Theatre building. From the makers of The Atrium (55/BEST RESTAUS) comes the latest Edin thing that might even have them dribbling into their Powerbooks in Soho. Furniture by Alasdair Gall and Tangram, design by Andrea Faed, best café-bar cooking in the city by a country mile. Blue is a light wood/metal/spacious establishment with a full menu from 12noon-3pm and 6pm-12midnight daily. Set snacks only in the afternoon, bar open to 1am daily. Minimal chic, maximal buzz.

CHP.INX

67
xE1

✝ ✝ **SKIPPERS:** 554 1018. 1a Dock Pl. In a corner of Leith off Commercial Rd by the docks. Look for Waterfront (*see below*) and bear left into adj cul-de-sac. The pioneer restaurant in the pre-yuppie Leith, it's still after all these yrs quite the best real bistro in town. V fishy, v quayside intimate and friendly. Look no further out to sea. Dinner: Tue-Sat, LO 10pm. MED

68
E4

✝ **HOWIE'S:** 668 2917. 75 St Leonard's St. Up on the S side, this extended set of rms is always busy. Unfussy, extensive and eclectic menu the epitome of good Edin bistro food that's affordable. Totally reliable and inexp eating out. Though this is the original Howie's, 2 others hit the same spot S and W of the city. 63 Dalry Rd, 313 3334. The best place to eat in the neighbourhood 100m up from Haymarket Stn. 208 Bruntsfield Pl, 221 1777. In a converted church. All 7 days lunch and dinner. LO 10/10.30pm. Cl Mon lunch. BYOB (with corkage) or unpretentious wine list.

INX

69
B3

✝ **INDIGO YARD:** 220 5603. 7 Charlotte Lane. Food in bar area and in restau upstairs in converted and glazed-over yard behind the W End. Enormously popular and always buzzing so you may not hear your wine pop or your cookie crumble. Earlier therefore better for conversational meals, but snackier supper menu from 10pm-1am is worth remembering. Food modern Med/Mex-Scottish and far better than café-bar standard. 7 days, lunch and evening menu LO 10pm, then supper. (293/THESE ARE HIP)

INX

THE WATERFRONT: 554 7427. 1c Dock Pl. In this foody corner of the waterfront, The Waterfront conservatory o/looks the backwater dock. It's *the* place to head in summer, but the warren of rms is cosy in winter. Food has wavered a bit over the yrs and now new ownership, but site and setting are mostly what you come for. Food update next time. 7 days, LO 10pm.   MED

70
xE1

 THE SHORE: 553 5080. 3 The Shore, Leith. Bar (often with live light jazz) where you can eat from the same menu as the dining-rm/restau. Real fire and large windows looking out to the Water of Leith. Food, listed on a blackboard, changes daily but is consistently good. Lots of fish, some meat, some vegn. No smk in restau/OK in bar. 7 days, LO 10pm. (276/PUB FOOD)   MED

71
xE1

 MALMAISON BRASSERIE AND CAFÉ MAL: 555 6969. Tower Pl at Leith dock gates. Restau and café-bar of Malmaison (10/INDIVIDUAL HOTELS). Authentic brasserie atmos and menu with linen cloths, big windows, steak frites. Café has lighter, more Mediterranean and vegn food. 7 days. Lunch and dinner. MED.INX

72
xE1

DANIEL'S: 553 5933. 88 Commercial Quay, off Dock Pl. Versatile with small deli, takeaway and bistro. Main eaterie is housed in new conservatory at back of old bonded warehouse. Clean lines, modern look and v popular. Offers contemporary French menu with Alsace and external influences that has been packing us in. Daniel himself is a gent and deserves to succeed. 7 days, 9am-10pm. INX

73
xE1

NICOLSON'S: 557 4567. 6a Nicolson St, opp Festival Theatre. An airy, blue-and-yellow first-floor eaterie – same owners as The Grain Store (134/SCOTTISH RESTAUS). Flexible menu offers everything from breakfast to post-theatre dinner. The cooking's competent, or you could always just waste a couple of hrs with a bottle of wine and a chum, but after 7pm the 'dinner' menu is more exp and they like you to eat. 9am-12midnight daily (216/LATE-NIGHT RESTAUS).   INX

74
D3

THE DORIC: 225 1084. 15 Market St. Opp the Fruitmarket Gallery and the back entrance to Waverley Stn. Upstairs bistro with chequered cloths, awful paintings, eclectic menu. Famous for their unaccommodating attitude to latecomers and the rude expulsion you get when they want to close the bar; and it ain't cheap any longer. All this aside it's still a gr bistro; we always go back. 7 days, LO 10.30pm.   MED

75
D3

76
D4

PIGS: 667 6676. 41 W Nicolson St. Edin does have a fair complement of bistros and although the important ones are mentioned above there are others worthy of note – like Pigs. Small, neat and sweet, the cooking dares to be different (Botswana meat stew) and you can BYOB. Won't win awards; has won fans. Lunch Mon-Sat, LO 10pm daily.   INX

77
D3

LE SEPT: 225 5428. 7 Old Fishmarket Close. The cobbled close winds steeply off the High St below St Giles. Wee o/side terrace in summer and narrow woody rm inside for nonsmokers (but smokey rm too). Crêpes, omelettes, plats du jour and Franco-bistro food. Cheerful, busy rendezvous with well-regarded staff. Mon-Thu lunch and LO 10.30pm; Fri 12noon-11.30pm; Sat 12noon-11pm; Sun 12.30-10.30pm.   INX

78
D3

THE DIAL: 225 7179. 44-46 George IV Br. Modern Scottish with an international spin in this subterranean designer eaterie. Drawbacks: curious Edin basement smell and question marks over the service. But then it looks cool, does a bargain pre-theatre menu and much effort has gone into the aesthetics, edible or otherwise. On balance: dial 225 7179.   MED

79
B1

MAISON HECTOR: 332 5328. 47 Deanhaugh St, Stockbridge. Designer revelation when it opened, getting shabbified, but still going strong. Coffee and muffins all day (nice cappuccino with Flake), lunch Mon-Fri, gr Sat/Sun brunch (225/SUNDAY BREAK-FAST) and decent dinner from 6-10.30pm daily. Or just go for a drink. Mirrored pissoir in the gents for the inquisitive or narcissistic. Bar Sun-Thu 10.30am-12midnight, Fri-Sat until 1am.   INX

80
C4

A ROOM IN MARCHMONT: 229 4404. 21 Argyle Pl. Exactly that, but an excellent neighbourhood bistro with dead cheap prices and BYOB. Seafood from legendary Eddie Tse's round the corner. Lunch Mon-Fri, dinner Mon-Sat. LO 10pm.   INX

CHAINS-U-LIKE

None of these may be too happy being described as a 'chain' but the bar/bistros have common owners and Pierre Victoire is everywhere.

MONTPELIERS: 229 3115. 159-161 Bruntsfield Pl. Food available at flexible times with that now-ubiquitious Med-Mex menu to the fore. Busy with better-heeled students, occasional footballers and the local, young bourgeoisie – so sometimes loud. 'Sympathy for the Devil' was playing when our researcher visited and he liked that. 9am-1am daily, LO dinner 10pm, supper menu until close. Same people have **INDIGO YARD** (69/BEST BISTROS) and **IGUANA** (295/THESE ARE HIP).

81
C4

THE CALEDONIAN ALEHOUSE/BISTRO: 337 1006. 1 Haymarket Terr, adj Haymarket Stn. Green leather and wood in the downstairs bar, well thought-out candlelit bistro upstairs where veggies needn't feel left out. A successful formula so the owners have also opened **THE CALEY BISTRO:** 622 7170. 30 Leven St, Tollcross. Good robust modern Scottish nr the King's Theatre. Lunch and LO 10.30pm daily. Meanwhile **EH1**: 220 5277, 197 High St, is perhaps the most stylish of the lot. Another breakfast/lunch/dinner café/eaterie. V blue and yellow – sit through the back and it feels like a balcony o/looking Cockburn St. Until 1am daily. Finally, **THE QUADRANT** in North Berwick is a nineties thing on an unfashionable coast.

82
A3, C3

PIERRE VICTOIRE: Apologies to Monsieur Levicky (proprietor) but the word that keeps coming up in conversations about his restaus these days is 'McDonalds'. With half a dozen PVs in Edin, another in South Queensferry and ten elsewhere in Scotland, this is no longer a happily unique wee Franco-bistro selling a bargain lunch. (And we're not counting other French, Italian and veggie spin-offs.) Foodies swap stories about how 'their' PV just isn't as good as it was, although this might be an example of that Scottish tendency to cry 'ah kent yer faither'. In the capital, the original restau (225 1721, 10 Victoria St) has a fine buzz and no elbow rm in the evenings, so still a fave and perhaps we're havering. The Leith outlet (5 Dock Pl, 555 6178) is v pop at lunch times – looking babelicious helps get you served. Also at 8 Union St (557 8451), 38-40 Grassmarket (226 2442), 17 Queensferry St (226 1890) and 8 Gloucester St, Stockbridge (225 1037).

83
D3

THE BEST FRENCH RESTAURANTS

84
C2

✠ **DUCK'S AT LE MARCHE NOIR:** 558 1608. 2-4 Eyre Pl. The Duck in question is not the edible sort, but proprietor Malcolm Duck who presides with meticulous attention to detail in his bistro/restau at the lower end of the New Town. In a residential neighbourhood, an easy-going but still business-like atmos. It may remind you of somewhere in France. Various *menus complets* to choose from, with some imaginative regional variations and regular gourmet evenings. Good-value wine list. Dinner 7 days, lunch Mon-Fri. LO 10.30pm (earlier Sun). MED

85
C2

✠ **CAFÉ SAINT-HONORÉ:** 226 2211. 34 Thistle St Lane, betw Frederick St and Hanover St. Fund managers, business dudes, New Town regulars and occasional lunching ladies all to be found in this busy, shiny bistro-cum-restau that smacks of *fin de siècle* Paris. If the Impressionists were alive, they'd be cadging desserts. International menu with v French flavour – veggies should phone ahead. EXP

86
C2

✠ **L'AUBERGE:** 556 5888. 58 St Mary's St. Proprietor Daniel Wencker pitched his *auberge* on St Mary's *rue* 20yrs ago when French cuisine ruled the world and places like this were culinary outposts. Now anywhere with a croissant on the menu can call itself a brasserie, but few real French restaus remain; this is one of them. The atmos is a tad formal but they know good service and they know good wine. *Quel dommage* that the food and presentation is so uncompromisingly bourgeois. Expected to go upmarket due to imminent proximity of the new Parliament (with all its power lunchbreaks). Sun lunch is popular. 7 days, LO 9.30 pm. EXP

87
C2

✠ **CHAMBERTIN:** 225 1251. 21 George St. Discreet, v professionally run main restau of George Hotel (9/BEST HOTELS) in opulent salon where suits dine at lunch time and retired members of the Edin establishment whinge about their grandkids. More relaxed in the evenings. Food has a welcome zing these days and there are unexpected *au courant* flourishes like translucent blue crockery that make for a pleasant clash with the décor. Lunch Mon-Fri, LO 10pm Mon-Sat. Cl Sun. EXP

88
D4

LA BONNE VIE: 667 1110. 49 Causewayside. Popular bistro in Edin's S side. V agreeable. Sitting among the garlands, stone walls, shining glassware and candles for a few mins, there's a growing sense of personality, then it hits you. This is the Felicity Kendall of capital restaus – and that's a compliment. Scottish produce, French outlook. Lunch and LO 10.30pm daily.   MED

JACQUES: 229 6080. 8 Gillespie Pl, Bruntsfield. Endearing French staff and endearing French typos – 'goast' cheese [*sic*] – make this a bistro to tug at your heartstrings. A hard-working wee rustic eaterie close to the King's Theatre, so well placed for pre-/post-show meals. Has all those French dishes – mussels, roulade – and throws in left-fielders like ostrich, yes, ostrich! Also Sun brunch. Good work you Gauls! Lunch and LO 11pm Mon-Sat, 10am-10pm Sun.   INX

89
C4

CHEZ JULES: 225 7007. 1 Craig's Close, off Cockburn St. Another chapter in the Pierre Victoire histoire with CJ bistros following PVs in every big town. Fairly similar – v French and pretty cheap. The restau feels subterranean, dishes on offer include pigeon, moules, onion soup, etc. Mon-Sat 6pm-11pm. Cl Sun. Also at 61 Frederick St for brighter surroundings, 225 7983. Mon-Sat 12noon-3pm then 6-11pm.   INX

90
D3

CAFÉ D'ODILE: 225 5366. 13 Randolph Cres. A secret grd and small cafeteria downstairs at the French Institute. Lunch only but can be booked for parties at night. Gr views over the New Town, simple French home-cooking, patronised by ladies who lunch. Terribly genteel, but occasional studenty BYOB types. Tue-Sat. Not licensed.   CHP

91
B2

LA POTINIÈRE: 01620 843214. Main St, Gullane. Report: 56/BEST RESTAUS.

MARINETTE: 555 0922. 52 Coburg St. Report: 113/SEAFOOD RESTAUS.

THE POMPADOUR: 459 9988. Caledonian Hotel, Princes St. Report: 62/BEST RESTAUS.

THE BEST ITALIAN RESTAURANTS

92
xE1

SILVIO'S: 553 3557. 54 The Shore. On the waterfront in Leith. Discreet frontage, deceptively low-key ristorante. This is excellent stuff. Classically simple, contemporary Italian/Mediterranean cuisine. Perfectly judged *antipasti* and invariably good fish and seafood of the day. Let them advise you. Some decent wines. Mon-Sat lunch and LO 10.30pm. No smk.   MED

93
B3

SCALINI: 220 2999. 10 Melville Pl. A new (1998) Silvio's (same owners) in the W End. Downstairs (the *scalini*) in a low-ceilinged sliver of a basement with a similar menu and approach. And they have the good Gattinara ('60, '70, '74, etc.). Same hrs as Silvio's (*see above*).   MED

94
B2

RAFFAELLI'S: 225 6060. 10 Randolph Pl, W End. Capital's worst-kept secret Italian? Hidden away in a lane behind W Register House at the back of Charlotte Sq this excellent restau is the kind of place where unit trust bods tell pals about villas nr Lucca. High standard of cooking, attentive service, strong Italian wine list, fairly formal. Lunch Mon-Fri, LO 10.30pm Mon-Sat. Cl Sun.   MED

95
E1

VALVONA & CROLLA: 556 6066. 19 Elm Row. The legendary deli now with café (rather than restau), but given manageress Carina Contini's care and attention, produce shipped in from Italy (fresh veg from Milan markets) and gr Italian domestic cooking on offer, this has been a big hit since it opened in spring 1996. Everything from vegn breakfast to fab lemon polenta cake and coffee for afternoon nibblers via a damned fine lunch. May be queues. No smk. Mon-Sat 8am-5pm. Not cheap, but clearly worth every penny.   INX

96
C2

COSMO: 226 6743. 58 N Castle St (a no through rd). V much in the old, discreet style for those with some time and cash on their hands. In Edin terms, has been the upmarket Italian restau for yrs and it is often fully booked. Famous people like Sean do get brought here. The lighting and the music are soft, the service impeccable and the (Italian) wine list exemplary. Menu pragmatically brief; allow time to enjoy it. 6 days. Cl Sun and Sat lunch.   EXP

97
D2

LIBRIZZI'S: 668 1997. 22a Nicolson St. Small basement ristorante opp Festival Theatre. The chef from Vito's (*see below*)

and Cosmo (*see above*) started up on his own, and this intimate and personal place is the result. Underrated, but reliable, esp for fish. Good service, well-selected wines. Cl Sun, LO 11pm.　　MED

✚ **TINELLI:** 652 1932. 139 Easter Rd. Small and neat restau with unassuming frontage on unfashionable st that was serving air-dried beef long before anyone else. Not a pizza/pasta joint – grilled liver with balsamic vinegar more their style. One of the city's best Italians. Lunch and LO 10.30pm Mon-Sat.　　MED

98
E1

✚ **VITO'S:** 225 5052. 55a Frederick St. Vito's has been in Edin for nigh on 20yrs, but this place seems as fresh and the menu as contemporary and Mediterranean as any. Basement rms are light but intimate and service is v good. They can always fit you in and get you sorted if you're in a hurry.　　MED

99
C2

TONY'S: 226 5877. 42 St Stephen St. Identifiable by the floral window box, this small tratt features a high standard of Italian cooking, comparable with the standard of patter from Tony himself. V popular so book. Daily, evenings only, LO 11pm. (Slightly larger restau at 19 Colinton Rd, 447 8781. Same menu, excellent service.)　　INX

100
C1

PEPE'S TAVERNA: 337 9774. 96 Dalry Rd. Taverna's just the word – checked tablecloths, dark wooden fixtures and hanging pots and pans. Food is standard Italian but when virtually everywhere else has packed up for the night, Pepe's keeps on keeping on. A Dalry haven 6pm-2.30am. Cl Tue. (220/LATE-NIGHT RESTAUS)　　INX

101
A4

GIULIANO'S: 556 6590. 18 Union Pl, top of Leith Walk nr the main r/bout, opp Playhouse Theatre. No change at Giuli's but something sets it apart as it's often heaving with happy punters. It's just pasta and pizza but in a no-nonsense manner that appeals. Lunch and LO 2am daily. Also another 'on the shore' in Leith (554 5272) which is esp good for kids (173/KID-FRIENDLY).　　INX

102
D2

BEPPE VITTORIO: 226 7267. 7 Victoria St. Italian peasant kitchen kinda thing from the makers of Pierre Victoire (83/CHAINS-U-LIKE) with reliable bistro-ish nosh. Informal and rustic feel which is gr if you're in the mood for excellent *linguine al pesto*. From 10am for coffee, lunch daily, LO Mon-Sat 11pm, Sun 10pm.　　INX

103
D3

DAL MARE: 555 0122. 76 Commercial St, Leith. Report: 115/SEAFOOD RESTAUS.

GORDON'S TRATTORIA: 225 7992. 231 High St. Report: 218/LATE-NIGHT RESTAUS.

BAR ROMA: 226 2977. 39a Queensferry St. Report: 219/LATE-NIGHT RESTAUS.

THE BEST PIZZA

Sometimes only pizza will do – here's where to go.

104
xE1

CAPRICE: 554 1279. 325-331 Leith Walk. Old-style – hip in the '70s and hasn't changed much. Pizzas fired up to order in a wood-burning oven, kitsch décor (ditto other menu items) but kids love it and it gets busy at peak times when families, couples and Leither Spice Girls come out to play. Lunch Mon-Sat, LO 11pm Mon-Thu, 11.30pm Fri-Sat, 10pm Sun. INX

105
B1

PIZZA EXPRESS: 332 7229. 1 Deanhaugh St, Stockbridge. Well-kent down S but Edin's brace only opened in '97. Stockbridge branch best, in refurbed bank with Water of Leith gurgling by. Simple, no-nonsense, affordable pizza with good service. Recent award for architecture. Edin W End branch, 225 8863, 32 Queensferry St. Both open until 12midnight daily. INX

106
C3

MAMMA'S: 225 6464. 30 Grassmarket. Brash, American-style with informal booking system (chalk your name on the board then nip off to the pub to wait). Some alternatives to pizza, but you really come to mix 'n' match – haggis, calamari and BBQ sauce only a sample of 44 toppings on offer. 12noon-10.30pm Sun-Thu, until 1am Fri-Sat (later if you're still eating). Also 1 Howard St, Canonmills. INX

107
E1

JOLLY: 556 1588. 9 Elm Row. Another wood-burning oven, pizzas as good as the Caprice (*see above*) but adorned with the wallpaper that time forgot. Nice staff. Take it away! INX

THE BEST RESTAURANTS FOR MEDITERRANEAN FOOD

✠ **IGG'S:** 557 8184. 15 Jeffrey St, nr Royal Mile. Maybe misleading to include Igg's here because although it serves the best tapas in town, they're only available at lunch. Overall, it's a v smart eaterie serving some of the best victuals in Edin – Spanish/Scots crossover. Excellent sauces and riojas. Other restau owners and notable Edinburgers eat here. Lunch; LO 10.30pm. Cl Sun.   MED

108
D3

TAPAS TREE: 556 7118. 1 Forth St. Bustling wee restau with upbeat Spanish staff and gypsy/Cajun soundtrack. Starter/main/pud is the heavier option but 3 well-chosen tapas (veg, fish and something else) with some robust bread and a bottle of house red makes for a v decent meal. Snappy service. Tapas in the £2 to £5 range, so not a pocket buster. 11am-10.30pm daily.   INX

109
D2

PHENECIA: 662 4493. 55-57 W Nicolson St, on corner nr Edin Univ. Unfussy yellow N African/Spanish eaterie with couscous, lots of grilled meats and wide vegn choice. Poss to eat v cheaply at lunch time – some people just pop in from that univ for hummus and salad. Lunch Mon-Sat, LO 11pm daily (10pm Sun). They have the Château Musar.   INX

110
D4

TAPAS OLÉ: 556 2754. 8-10 Eyre Pl. Newish (late '97) tapas restau/bar way down in the New Town. Meat/vegn/seafood menus and the usual vinos. Spacious rather than cosy with Spanish proprietor and waiters. Live music on Sun. 7 days lunch and LO 10 pm.   INX

111
C2

SILVIO'S: 553 3557. 54 The Shore, and **SCALINI:** 220 2999. 10 Melville Pl (92/93/ITALIAN RESTAUS).

THE BEST SEAFOOD RESTAURANTS

112
xE1

♱ ♱ **SKIPPERS:** 554 1018. 1a Dock Pl, Leith. Bistro with truly maritime atmos; mainly seafood. Best to book. Many would argue Skippers *is* the best place to eat seafood in town. Full report: 67/BEST BISTROS.

113
xD1

♱ **MARINETTE:** 555 0922. 52 Coburg St. My favourite seafood dining-rm on the other rd that leads to Leith. More *épatant* than anywhere else in the pt; you do find sailors and working girls, but not Simone Signoret sitting alone at the corner table with a fag. Straightforward ideal menu: mainly whatever fish is best of the day (bream, halibut and always monkfish) with a choice of sauces like ginger and coriander, served with *the* best bowl of chips in town. There are other options which the irrepressible Francis will advise; he will certainly be on your case (unobtrusive he ain't). Tue-Sat lunch, dinner. LO 10pm. MED

114
xE1

♱ **FISHERS:** 554 5666. Corner of The Shore and Tower St, Leith. At the foot of an 18th-century tower opp Malmaison Hotel and rt on the quay (though no boats come by). Seafood cooking with flair and commitment in boat-like surroundings where trad Scots dishes get an imaginative twist. V good indeed. Cheeseboard has some gr Brits if you have rm for a third course. Clientele can tend towards self-consciously chic types; impeccable staff working from galley kitchen deserve big tips. 7 days. 12noon-10.30pm. MED

115
xE1

DAL MARE: 555 0722. Commercial St, Leith. On the 'quay' in restau row, an authentic Italian job specialising in fish and seafood. Antonio Iannozzi arrived with his team from southern Italy, bedecked in the prestigious Green Ribbon (for light cuisine) in late 1997. Décor is sand 'n' surf; food is surf 'n' token turf, incl veal, as the Italians do. Excellent vinos. Lunch and LO 11pm. Cl Sun. MED

116
D3

CREELERS: 220 4447. 3 Hunter Sq. Tim and Fran James still have their excellent seafood restau and smokehouse in Arran, also called Creelers, and Tim somehow still manages to go fishing. But mainly they work damned hard in their corner of the revamped Hunter Sq behind the Tron Church, just a short cast from the Royal Mile (tables alfresco in summer) to make this one of the best seafood spots in town. Nice paintings, good atmos, not exp. Bar meals at front, restau at back. Lunch and LO 10.30/11pm (cl Sun in winter). MED

CAFÉ ROYAL OYSTER BAR: 556 4124. W Register St. A place for a flourish of insanity or sheer exhibitionism. Beluga caviar followed by Homard Newburg with a bottle of Bolly came to £154 for 2 at last count. But you can also snack. Higher celeb quotient than most Edin restaus (Souness and Connolly when they're in town) there for the classy surroundings with spillover atmos from adj bar. Tiles, linen, dark wood, v Victorian. Visitors usually find it all v groovy; some locals lament that it ain't what it was. Lunch and LO 10.15pm daily. **117** **D2** EXP

BIG FISH AT THE FRUITMARKET GALLERY: 226 1843. Market St, behind the big windows. About to open at time of going to press (so no cross-reference number), James Robb's catch-of-the-night place bound to emulate the success of his daytime café (181/BEST TEA-ROOMS). Edin's chattering classes will be netted in and displayed, perhaps by candlelight, as you're rushing for your train. **D3** MED

THE BEST FISH 'N' CHIPS

✠ **L'ALBA D'ORO:** Henderson Row, nr corner with Dundas St. Large selection of deep-fried goodies, incl many vegn savouries. Inexp proper pasta, real pizzas and even the wine's OK. A lot more than your usual fry-up – as several plaques on the wall attest (incl *Scotland the Best!*). Open until 12midnight. **118** **D1** CHP

✠ **THE RAPIDO:** 77 Broughton St. Fine chips. Popular with late-nighters stumbling back down the hill to the New Town, and the flotsam of the 'Pink Triangle'. Open until 1.30am (3.30am Fri-Sat). **119** **D2** CHP

✠ **THE DEEP SEA:** Leith Walk, opp Playhouse. Open late and often has queues but these are quickly dispatched. The haddock has to be 'of a certain size'. Trad menu. Still one of the best fish suppers you'll ever feed a hangover with. Open until 2am(-ish) (3am Fri-Sat). **120** **D2** CHP

THE BEST VEGETARIAN RESTAURANTS

121
D3

✠ **BLACK BO'S:** 557 6136. 57 Blackfriars St. Unlike other eateries below, this is a restau, not a way of life, that just so happens to be meatless, so none of your worthy veg crumble here – almond and potato terrine more their thing. Adventurous use of fruit in main dishes, although proprietors fed up being described as 'fruity'. Adj bar (279/PUB FOOD) now offers similar standard of cooking during the day, restau open evenings only, LO 10.30pm daily.   INX

122
D4

✠ **KALPNA:** 667 9890. 2-3 St Patrick Sq. Long-established vegn restau which is also something else – a good Indian one – so more interesting than many. Thali gives a good overview while bargain Wed buffet features regional cuisine. No smk. Lunch Mon-Fri, dinner 7 days, LO 10.30pm (10pm Sun). (143/INDIAN RESTAUS)   INX

123
D4

✠ **ANN PURNA:** 662 1807. 45 St Patrick Sq. Excellent vegn restau nr Edin Univ with genuine Gujerati/S Indian cuisine. Good atmos – old customers are greeted like friends. Indian beer, some suitable wines. Lunch Mon-Fri, dinner 7 days, LO 11pm. (144/INDIAN RESTAUS)   INX

124
D3

✠ **BANNS:** 226 1112. 5 Hunter Sq, just off Royal Mile at the Tron Church. Veggie burgers, Mexicana and many less predictable things in this informal eaterie on a redeveloped corner of the Old Town which has a performance space, making it a good place to eat alfresco in summer. Snacks and full meals all day, some vegan. Organic wines and beers, decent coffee from Gaggia machine and Pâtisserie Florentin desserts. Daily 10am-11pm.   INX

125
C2

✠ **HENDERSON'S:** 225 2131. 94 Hanover St. Edinburgh's original and trail-blazing basement vegn self-serve café-cum-wine bar. Canteen seating to the left (avoid), candles and live piano or guitar downstairs to the rt (better). Happy wee wine list and bottles of some excellent organic real ales. Good cheese. Cl Sun. LO 10pm. Also has the Farm Shop upstairs with a deli and takeaway and the more bar-like Henderson's Thistle Bistro round the corner in Thistle St.   CHP

126
D4

✠ **SUSIE'S DINER:** 667 8729. 51-53 W Nicolson St. Formerly Seeds, this vegn/vegan diner now boasts a more varied menu with Mexican and Middle-Eastern dishes, occasional live music and belly dancing nights, so less po-faced than its predecessor (hurrah). But could they please abandon tofu 'cheesecake'? Licensed, also BYOB. Mon 9am-9pm, Tue-Sat 9am-10pm. Cl Sun.

CHP

ENGINE SHED CAFÉ: 662 0040. 19 St Leonard's Lane. Hidden away off St Leonard's St, this is a lunch-oriented vegn café where much of the work is done by adults with learning difficulties on training placements, so worth supporting. Simple, decent food and gr bread – baked on premises, for sale separately. Nice stopping-off point after a tramp over Arthur's Seat. (Also has a shop at 123 Bruntsfield Pl.) Mon-Thu 10.30am-3.30pm, Fri 10.30am-2.30pm, Sat 10.30am-4pm, Sun 11.30am-4pm.

127
E4

CHP

HELIOS FOUNTAIN: 229 7884. 7 Grassmarket. Old hippies eat sugar-free cake, their kids play with building blocks and browsers check out the tenets of Steinerism (Rudolf, not George). Reliable self-service vegn caff, anthroposophical bookshop and gewgaw emporium. No smk. Mon-Sat 10am-6pm, Sun 12noon-4pm.

128
C3

CHP

CORNERSTONE CAFÉ: 229 0212. Underneath St John's Church at the corner of Princes St and Lothian Rd. V central and PC self-service coffee shop in church vaults. Home-baking and hot dishes at lunch time. Some seats outside in summer (in graveyard!) and market stalls during the Festival. One World Shop adj is full of Third World-type crafts and v good for presents. A respite from the fast-food frenzy of Princes St. Open 9.30am-4pm (later in Festival). Cl Sun.

129
C3

CHP

ISABEL'S: 662 4014. 83 Clerk St (in basement of Nature's Gate wholefood shop). V small café selling vegn standards. Pop in some time. Mon-Sat 11.30am-6.30pm.

130
E4

CHP

THE BEST SCOTTISH RESTAURANTS

131
C2

✝ ✝ **WINTER GLEN:** 477 7060. 3a1 Dundas St, which is on the rt going downhill opp the Scottish Gallery. Comfortable, intimate basement restau, and above a private dining-rm. Pleasing name comes not from sentiment, but from the surnames of the owners. Nevertheless this mainly Scottish menu originates from glen and loch and bay; Scotland's first-class ingredients featured and presented to exemplary effect. Smart service, urbane atmos without the ennui. The sort of restau you'd hope to find in the capital of a European country (quietly confident of its own cuisine). 6 days. Cl Sun and Sat lunch. MED

132
D3

✝ **DUBH PRAIS:** 557 5732. 123b High St. Slap bang (but downstairs) on the Royal Mile opp the Holiday Inn. Only 9 tables and a miniature galley kitchen from which proprietor/chef James McWilliams and his team produce a remarkably reliable à la carte menu from sound and sometimes surprising Scottish ingredients. Remarkable and surprising because you might not expect the largely suburban clientele to feast so enthusiastically on ostrich or rabbit, but they do. Testimony to the chef; there are many more conventional options. An outpost of culinary integrity on the Royal Mile. Cl Sun-Mon and Sat lunch. LO 10.30pm. MED

133
D2, C3

STAC POLLY: 229 5405. 8a Grindlay St. Opp Lyceum Theatre and not far from Usher Hall, Traverse and cinemas. Those haggis filo parcels that divide opinion are still on the menu which is largely local produce cooked up a storm (Scottish beef, salmon, game). The restau – dark wood and tartan curtains – is quietly smart. Cheeses come from Iain Mellis. There's another basement **STAC POLLY** at 29-33 Dublin St in the New Town (556 2231). Similar menu but it feels clubbier. V fine. Both: lunch Mon-Fri and LO 11pm Mon-Sat. Dublin St also open Sun evening to 11pm. MED

134
D3

THE GRAIN STORE: 225 7635. 30 Victoria St. Regulars come for the pigeon, salmon or guinea fowl – perhaps the vegn alternative – then hang around this laid-back first-floor eaterie drinking wine or coffee. Informal and welcoming, there are few better places for a relaxed Sun lunch extending far into the afternoon. More 'mod Brit' than simply 'Scottish' but this fine restau just has to fit in the book somewhere. Lunch and dinner daily, LO 11pm (10pm Sun). MED

HALDANE'S: 556 8407. 39 Albany St. In basement of The Albany (14/INDIVIDUAL HOTELS) New venture for the Kelsos from award-winning Ardsheal House at Kentallan. Restau is Scottish by nature rather than hype. Everything done in a country house style, down to the bar snacks. Best salmon starter in the capital? Lunch Mon-Fri, LO 9.30pm daily.

135
D2

MED

FENWICK'S: 667 4265. 15 Salisbury Pl. Peter Fenwick opened this bistro in late 1996, long overdue for an area like Newington. The cooking, with assorted international manoeuvres, offers local produce turned out with a goodly degree of style and honesty. If the kitchen drops the polenta underlay to your trout, the waitress will come and explain the delay. Affordable wine list chalked up on the wall. Lunch and LO 10.30pm Tue-Sat. Cl Sun-Mon.

136
xE4

INX

THE BEST MEXICAN RESTAURANTS

137
D3

✝ **VIVA MEXICO:** 226 5145. Anchor Close, Cockburn St. Has it really been here 13yrs? That says something about its position among the come-and-go Mexicans. Still throws in something innovative now and again, although all the expected dishes are here. Reliable venue for those times when nothing else fits the mood but sour cream, tacos and limey lager; nice atmos downstairs. Another branch nr Tollcross at 50 E Fountainbridge. Lunch (not Sun) and LO 10.30pm. INX

138
C2

TEX MEX: 225 1796. 47 Hanover St. Young, dumb and full of, er, tequila. A primal scream of a place in the city centre with all the usual Mexican faves, José Cuervo experiments and jolly soundtrack. Probably the best appointed of its ilk in Edin; infinitely preferable to others nearby. Slammersville. 12noon-1am Mon-Sat, until 12midnight Sun. INX

139
E4

MOTHER'S: 662 0772. 107-109 St Leonard's St. Gr wee neighbourhood restau that manages to do the basics well (unlike many other Tex/Mexicans in town). Burgers, beef, burritos and one or two departures like Cajun veggie kebabs. Simple décor, good staff, proper coffee, home-made desserts. A hit, a palpable hit. Dinner 6-10pm Tue-Thu and Sun, 6-10.30pm Fri-Sat. Cl Mon. INX

140
E3

PANCHO VILLA'S: 557 4416. 240 Canongate. This spartan cantina remains a reliable exponent of what we've come to regard as Mexican cooking with nosh of the 'chilada, 'ajita, 'ichanga school. Plain décor, decent edibles, happy place. Lunch 12noon-2.30pm Mon-Sat, dinner 6-10.30pm daily. INX

THE BEST INDIAN RESTAURANTS

✠ **SURUCHI:** 556 6583. 14a Nicolson St. Upstairs opp Festival Theatre. Owner from Jaipur called Mr Rodriguez plus chefs from Bengal, Delhi and S India equals eclectic Indian menu. Unfussy décor and food with light touch (good coconut rice) attracts students/academics from nearby univ as well as theatregoers. This place is routinely praised to the skies; we agree. Live music some nights. Lunch and LO 11.30pm daily.   INX

141
D3

THE RAJ: 553 3980. 89 Henderson St on S corner of The Shore, Leith. Take a certain amount of care with the food, add Tommy Miah's marketing nous and wadda-you-get? The most successful Indian/Bangladeshi restau in town. Regular events (Bangladeshi New Year and Food/Culture Fest) add to the jollity; jars of things available to buy and take home, also recipe books. Sun-Thu still does food 'at 1983 prices'. Try to sit up on the raised front area – better than the back. Totally Raj, in the non-Irvine Welsh sense. Lunch and LO 11.30pm, 7 days.   INX

142
xE1

KALPNA: 667 9890. 2-3 St Patrick Sq. The original Edin Indian veggie restau and still ragingly popular. Lighter, fluffier and not as attritional as so many tandooris. Wed buffet quite a bargain. Report: 122/VEGN RESTAUS.   INX

143
B1

ANN PURNA: 662 1807. 45 St Patrick Sq. Friendly and family-run Gujerati/S Indian veggie restau with seriously value-for-money business lunch. Report: 123/VEGN RESTAUS.   INX

144
B1

LANCERS: 332 3444. 5 Hamilton Pl. Bengali/N Indian, off busy Hamilton Pl in Stockbridge/New Town area. A 'Brits in India, those were the days' type restau (please may this go out of style soon) which can mean service on the precious side, but the food speaks for itself. Dining area not so comfortable, but New Townies with lovely kitchens do phone for a kerry-oot. 7 days. LO 11pm.   INX

145
B1

INDIAN CAVALRY CLUB: 228 3282. Athol Pl, W End, just off the main Glas rd, about 250m from Princes St. Bargain business lunch attracts the suits and another restau you'll like if you go for the retro colonial style. We don't esp – but no quibbles about the food. This seems an unlikely carry-out place, but they do and it's one of *the* best in town. Lunch and LO 11.30pm daily.   INX

146
B3

147
xE4

MOTHER INDIA: 662 9020. 10 Newington Rd. Capital invaded by Weegie pakora merchants shock! MI has branched out from its native Glas to offer Edimbourgeois fresh-made pakora/snacks in the bar as well as a full monty restau space (adj and upstairs). Food good in that Indo-wegian style; pakora fab. Odd collision of student diner intent in premises that used to house one of the city's swankiest Indians (the late Jaipur Mansion). Dinner LO 10.30 pm (lunch Fri only).   CHP.INX

148
C4

SHAMIANA: 228 2265. 14 Brougham St, Tollcross. Recommended by everyone from Egon Ronay (not a recommendation we'd rely on) to Gordon Brown, a prominent sign outside proclaims, 'Voted Best Restau in Scotland'. Well, up to a point Lord Copper. Small eaterie with quiet décor and v popular after rough patch. The food's good again, the kulcha is fine; the staff could lighten up a bit.   MED

149
D4

KEBAB MAHAL: 667 5214. 7 Nicolson Sq. Nr Edin Univ and Festival Theatre. Gr vegetable biryani and delicious lassi for under a fiver? Hence high cult status. Late-night Indo-Pakistani halal caff that attracts Asian families as well as students and others who know. Kebabs, curries and sweets. Sun-Thu 12noon-12midnight, Fri-Sat 12noon-2am. No alcohol.   CHP

150
D3

KUSHI'S: 556 8996. 16 Drummond St. Long regarded as another cult classic, this basic Punjabi café (no restau twiddly bits) has been drawing in students and others for cheap eats since Nehru was in nappies, or at least in the news. It's just round the corner from Edin Univ's Old College. Short no-nonsense menu, cheap no-nonsense prices. Unique, this is the stripped-down curry. Lunch Mon-Sat, dinner Mon-Thu 5-9pm, Fri-Sat 5-9.30pm. Cl Sun.   CHP

THE BEST FAR-EASTERN RESTAURANTS

SIAM ERAWAN: 226 3675. 48 Howe St. On corner of Stockbridge area, the first proper Thai in town and still much enjoyed – manages that quiet Eastern elegance v well. Same people also have **ERAWAN EXPRESS,** 220 0059, 176 Rose St, a kind of Thai canteen but not quite as inspired as its big sis, although it's early days yet. Both establishments lunch Mon-Sat, dinner daily, LO 11pm.

151
C2

AYUTTHAYA: 556 9351. 14b Nicolson St, opp Festival Theatre. Decent prospect pre- or post-show. Long, thin, not atmos restau, but attentive service, good vegn selection and a steady hand in the kitchen. Under the same ownership is **SUKHOTHAI:** 229 1537. 23 Brougham Pl, Tollcross. Funkier eaterie where the waitresses do their best to look delicate but would perhaps feel better in baseball caps. Sip your Singha – think not of Phuket. LO 10pm.   INX

152
D3

DARUMA-YA: 554 7660. 82 Commercial St (entry via Dock Pl). Japanese dining in the capital has a history of high prices and high snob value but at last one that is affordable. Bargain set meals. Frequented by execs from W Lothian firms like Mitsubishi – says it all really. Lunch Tue-Sat, LO 10.30pm Mon-Sat. Cl Sun.   MED

153
xE1

YUMI: 337 2173. 2 W Coates (continues from Haymarket Terr, W End). The classier and more polite of the capital's Japanese restaus. Our researcher thought it the cleanest rip in town.   EXP

154
xA3

SINGAPURA: 538 7878. 69 N Castle St, corner of Queen St. Mainly Malaysian and Singaporean cuisine, which seems to mean from anywhere E of Suez. So there's a bit of Thai, Indonesian and even Chinese. Fish and tempe for vegns. Lunch Mon-Sat, dinner daily. LO 10.30pm (11pm Fri-Sat).   INX

155
C2

THE KRIS: 556 6758. 20a Leopold Pl, London Rd. Odd setup. Malaysian restau in basement of unrelated and unremarkable hotel. At breakfast (8-10am daily) it serves trad Brit-grub and early-morning body fiends from Edinburgh Club gym next door pop in for a bacon roll. Later the assorted gorengs come out to play. Genuinely different. Lunch Sun-Fri, LO 10pm daily.   INX

156
E2

TAMPOPO: 220 5254. 25a Thistle St. Not a restau at all but a gr wee Japanese noodle bar where you can pick up a ramen to go or one of those meal on a tray things. Open lunch Mon-Sat, also 6-9pm Tue-Sat. Cl Sun.   CHP

157
C2

THE BEST CHINESE RESTAURANTS

158
C2

KWEILIN: 557 1875. 19 Dundas St. Large New Town place with imaginative Cantonese cooking (real chefs); v good seafood and genuine dim sum in pleasant but somewhat uninspired setting. No kids allowed in the evening – somewhere for grown-ups to eat their quail in peace. Book. 7 days, LO 10.45pm. MED

159
E4

DRAGON WAY: 668 1328. 74 S Clerk St. First thing that hits you as you go in – a big lacquer dragon wrapped around a pillar. Décor gloriously OTT and often described as 'Hollywood film set'. Good food mind you, and service, so one of the more interesting Chinese nights out. Lunch Mon-Fri and LO 10.30pm. INX

160
C1

LOON FUNG: 556 1781. 2 Warriston Pl, Canonmills. Upstairs (and down when it's crowded) the famous lemon chicken and crispy duck go round for ever. And damned fine seaweed. LO 11.30pm (Sun-Thu), 12.30am (Fri-Sat). **LOON FUNG:** 229 5757. 32 Grindlay St, opp Lyceum Theatre is a sister restau with seafood. INX

161
C3

ORIENTAL DINING CENTRE: 221 1288. 8 Morrison St, opp cinema complex. It's a restau (Rainbow Arch), a dim sum basement bar and a late-night noodle shack (**HO HO MEI** – cash only, eat in or take-away). Noodles 5.30pm-2.30am Mon-Sat. The restau is best by far in this neck of the W End. 12noon-11.30pm daily. INX

162
B3

LUNE TOWN: 220 1688. 38 William St. The wee one hidden away behind the W End with porcelain figurines in the window. Often busy, predominantly Cantonese nosh. Lunch and LO 11.30pm Mon-Fri. Open 3pm-12midnight Sat-Sun. MED

163
B3

NEW EDINBURGH RENDEZVOUS: 225 2023. 10a Queensferry St. Hardly new and easy to miss (upstairs, next door to travel agents). Functional décor, short wine list to be taken seriously and dishes you won't find in any other Scottish Chinese restaus: e.g shredded sea blubber. Lunch and LO 11pm Mon-Sat, 1-11pm Sun. INX

164
C4

LEE ON: 229 7732. 3-5 Bruntsfield Pl. Through purple porthole-effect windows, a restau popular with the Chinese community. Feels a bit *Man From UNCLE*, but food fine. Lunch Mon-Sat 12noon-2pm, LO 12midnight Sun-Thu, 1am Fri-Sat. INX

165
E1

YEE KIANG: 554 5833. 42 Dalmeny St. Peking home cooking courtesy of Johnny Wong deep in the heart of Hibbie land – feels like someone's living rm. Small, democratic. Does a mean fried crispy greens. An inside track choice. Tue-Sun 5-11.30pm. Cl Mon. INX

THE BEST RESTAURANTS FOR BURGERS AND STEAKS

✠ ✠ **CHAMPANY'S:** 01506 834532. On A904, Linlithgow to S Queensferry rd (3km Linlithgow), but nr M9 at jnct 3. Accolade-laden restau (and 'Chop and Ale House') different from others below because it's out of town (and out of most pockets). Both surf 'n' turf with live lobsters on premises. Good service, huge helpings (Americans may feel at home). Chop House 7 days, lunch and LO 10pm; restau lunch (not Sat) and LO 10pm. Cl Sun. INX.EXP

166
xA2

✠ **BELL'S DINER:** 225 8116. 7 St Stephen St, Stockbridge. Bill Allan's almost-legendary small American diner actually predates the New Town (only kidding Bill). But it's been there a long time; an Edin reference pt. Successful formula with gr burgers and steaks to the fore, but veggies need not avoid – the best nutburger in town with mustard, roquefort, etc. Staff are pretty cool too. Mon-Fri 6-10.30pm, Sat-Sun 12noon-10.30pm. INX

167
C1

✠ **THE ROCK:** 555 2225. Commercial St, Leith. Where to go for lunch with clients or dinner out when all you want is a steak/burger and chips (there are other options). Best in town. Report: 64/BEST RESTAUS.

168

SMOKE STACK: 556 6032. 53-55 Broughton St. From the makers of The Basement (245/GREAT EDIN PUBS) comes something across the rd – a burgundy and blue diner rather than an orange and blue café-bar. Modish décor has a soothing effect. Loads of burgers (Scottish beef or vegn), seared salmon, etc. jollied along by a gr staff. (Santana at lunch time, just like old times.) Proper menu available lunch and dinner, but food of some sort all day. Also does a good Sun brunch (228/SUNDAY BREAKFAST). Open 12noon-10.30pm daily. INX

169
D2

WIGWAM: 225 6127. 64 Thistle St. Bright colours in this central, but backstreet Native Americana diner. Mainly meat – a buffalo wings kinda joint – but vegn burgers too, with a good guacamole. Tex-Mex obviously, handy business lunch venue. Lunch and LO 11pm daily. INX

170
C2

BUFFALO GRILL: 667 7427. 12-14 Chapel St. Burn that beef! Although this diner trades on its reputation for steaks and suchlike, there are some Mexican concessions to veggies. Not big, so book and BYOB if you want. Lunch Mon-Fri, LO 10.15pm (Sun 10pm). INX

171
E4

KID-FRIENDLY PLACES

172
xE1

✠ **UMBERTO'S:** 554 1314. Bonnington Rd Lane off Bonnington Rd to E of Newhaven Rd jnct. Whitewashed coach house hidden away in a v unlikely part of Leith. In contrast to some other 'kiddie' places, grown-ups would actually want to eat here too. Downstairs is a civilised restau, upstairs a theme area for kids where some booths form part of a big toy train and mobile young-sters can run in and out of the Wendy house. Upstairs open Mon-Fri 12noon-2pm then 5-7.30pm, Sat 12noon-7.30pm, Sun 12noon-5.30pm. Downstairs lunch and LO 10pm Mon-Sat.   INX

173
xE1

✠ **GIULIANO'S ON THE SHORE:** 554 5272. 1 Commercial St by the br. With its checked tablecloths, accented waiters and cheerful pizza/pasta menu, this is almost a cartoon version of an Italian restau – no slight intended – and kids love it. Always a birthday party happening at w/ends. Lunch and LO 10.30/11pm.   INX

174
xC1

YE OLDE PEACOCK INN: 552 8707. Newhaven Rd nr Newhaven Harbour and opp Harry Ramsden's (a more obvious place to take kids perhaps, *see below*), but this has been one of Edin's unsung all-round family eateries for yrs, and deserves wider recognition. The fish here really is fresh, the menu is more adventurous than you'd think with lots that wee kids and we kids like. High tea is a treat. Lunch and LO 9.30pm Mon-Thu, 12noon-9.30pm Fri-Sun.   CHP

175
B3

FAT SAM'S: 228 3111. 56 Fountainbridge. Cavernous gr Italian-style barn with a couple of enormous television screens, fish tank and animatronic cartoon-like Fat Sam to scare the unwary. The scale and sheer chutzpah appeal to children of all ages (i.e. stu-dents' night out). Kids' menu has usual burgers, pizzas and all that jazz. Main menu has all that's jazzier (swordfish, gnocchi) but really a place for the young at heart and brain.   INX

176
xA4

BRIDGE INN, RATHO: 333 1320. Canal Centre, Ratho, W Lothian. 14km W of centre via A71, turning rt opp Dalmahoy Golf Club. Well worth the drive for an afternoon on, or by, the Union Canal. The Pop Inn Restau has special menus for kids, play areas and numerous distractions. Sailings and walks. (289/PUB FOOD) LO food 9pm, bar open 12noon-11pm (12midnight Fri-Sat).   INX

177
xA2

CRAMOND BRIG HOTEL: 339 4350. At the R Almond as you hit Edin on the dual carriageway from the Forth Rd Br. This inn has put a lot of effort into attracting families with its indoor/outdoor play areas (Funky Forest). If you've driven for hrs with a whingeing child and want steak and chips while wee Daniel or Amy play themselves into a stupor then it's v convenient. Otherwise a bit characterless. Lunch and LO 9.30pm, 7 days. Open from lunch straight through to close on Sat-Sun. INX

HUNTER'S TRYST: 445 3132. 97 Oxgangs Rd. Adj to Safeway, corner of Oxgangs Rd N. Big steaks in the boonies. If this place was another half mile S it would be up the Pentlands so a long schlep from town – but nr Fairmilehead exit from bypass, so happy for travellers. Alloa's bid for kid-friendliness sees a bright Wacky Warehouse play area (it is a warehouse and it's v wacky) connected to pub/inn selling pub/inn food. WW closes 7pm Mon-Wed, 9pm Thu-Sun. Inn until 11pm daily, LO food 9pm (snacks until close). INX

178
xC4

HARRY RAMSDEN'S: 551 5566. Newhaven Rd. Edin branch of national chain. Bright, tacky, predictable menu, but nice location by harbour with seats o/side. All day, 7 days. CHP

179
xA1

THE BEST TEAROOMS AND COFFEE SHOPS

180
xA2

GALLERY OF MODERN ART CAFÉ: Belford Rd. Utterly unbeatable on a fine day when you can sit out on the patio by the grass, with sculptures around, have some wine and a plate of Scottish cheese and oatcakes. Hot dishes are excellent. Coffee and cake whenever. Then it's back upstairs for the art. Oh well! Mon-Sat 10am-4.30pm, Sun 2-4.30pm. (338/OTHER ATTRACTIONS)

181
D3

FRUITMARKET CAFÉ: 226 1843. 29 Market St. Attached to the Fruitmarket Gallery, a cool spacious place for coffee, cake or a light lunch courtesy of James Robb. Big windows to look out; good mix of tourists, Edin faithfuls and art seekers – the latter go upstairs. Mon-Sat 10.30am-5.30pm, Sun 12noon-5pm.

182
D2

QUEEN STREET CAFÉ: National Portrait Gallery (337/OTHER ATTRACTIONS), Queen St betw Hanover and St Andrew's Sq. And through the arched window . . . a civil slice of old Edin gentility. Serving seriously good light meals, tasteful sandwiches, coffee and cake – best scones in town, among other things. Mon-Sat 10am-4.30pm, Sun 2-4.30pm.

183
D3

CAFÉ FLORENTIN: 225 6267. 8 St Giles St. Have turned an entire generation of Edimbourgeois on to almond croissants and wicked tartelettes. Uptown café with downtown décor, this establishment is the capital in a nutshell (or shortcrust pastry case). Advocates rub shoulders with student grunge queens over a blast of caffeine. Open 7am-11pm daily (2am Fri-Sat), really late during the Festival. Also at 5 NW Circus Pl, Stockbridge – with shop, 7am-7pm daily. And next to the Lyceum Theatre, Grindlay St, though we think this one has been a *pont* too far. (223/SUNDAY BREAKFAST)

184
C2

LAIGH KITCHEN: 225 1552. 117a Hanover St. Truly Scotland. Fundamental, friendly and 40-something; a basement coffee howf (Neil Grant the hairdresser is upstairs) with unimpeachable cakes, wooden seats and tables on a stone floor. Gr salads. Some folk live in the city for yrs and hardly notice it – others wouldn't go anywhere else. A true gem. Mon-Sat 8.30am-4pm.

185
C4

KAFFE POLITIK: 446 9873. 146-148 Marchmont Rd. All black and white and wood and middle-Euro chic at another converted bank in the heart of student flat land. Rear wall speckled with quotes from assorted celebs – Indira Gandhi to Woodrow Wilson. Damn fine cup of coffee, sodas, juice, soup 'n' sandwiches. Small choice of v good breakfasts (224/SUNDAY BREAKFAST). 10am-10pm daily.

KINNELLS: 220 1150. 36 Victoria St. Stone and distressed tartan and aged – in an elegant way. A characteristic capital hideaway for wet and dry days. Some tables downstairs in the shop where they sell a big range of teas and coffees – but best to go up. Light meals, cake and good cheese. 10am-6pm daily (later during the Festival). Takeaway next door open Mon-Sat 10am-4pm.

186
D3

SEATTLE COFFEE COMPANY: 226 3610. 128 Princes St, 2nd floor of Waterstone's bookshop. Dare we say better than the cramped original at London's Covent Garden? Easily. In among the books, a young and friendly staff dispense everything from caffè latte to iced Americano. Savouries and pâtisserie courtesy of Pâtisserie Florentin (*see above*). View of the Castle. Open 9.30am-8pm Mon-Sat, 11am-5pm Sun. Another more business-like branch in the basement of the Edin Solicitors Property Centre at 85 George St – a more stand-alone branch to open in spring '98 in Lothian Rd.

187
C3

CLARINDA'S: 557 1888. 69 Canongate. Nr the bottom of the Royal Mile nr the Palace (and the soon-to-be Parliament). A small tearoom with hot dishes and snacks that may seem more of a sit-down stop on the tourist trail but actually has prob the best home-baking in town (esp the apple pie). V reasonable prices; run by good Edin folk. 10am-4.45pm (from 12noon Sun).

188
E2

THE ELEPHANT HOUSE: 220 5355. 21 George IV Br. Nr libraries and Edin Univ, a rather self-conscious but big-time and well-run coffee shop with light snacks and multifarious choice of caffeines and tannins to speed your research. Cakes/pastries are bought in but can be taken out. Mon-Fri 8am-11pm, Sat-Sun 10am-11pm.

189
D3

COMMON GROUNDS: 226 1416. 2-3 N Bank St, top of The Mound. The kind of coffee emporium where tourists wander in by accident and women can breast feed with impunity. Cake, light meals, insane range of espressos incl the 'Keith Richards' (a quadruple). Live music some nights. 9am-10pm, Sat-Sun from 10am.

190
D3

G&T (GLASS & THOMPSON): 557 0909. 2 Dundas St. Patrician New Town coffee shop and deli with contemporary food and attitude. Staff Like Us serve portions of spinach and nutmeg pâté discussing

191
C2

Roman hols. Gr *antipasti*, salads and sandwiches to go. 8.30am-6.30pm, Sat until 5.30pm, Sun 11am-4.30pm. (231/TAKEAWAYS)

192
B1

BOTANIC GARDENS CAFETERIA: By 'the House' (where there are regular exhibs), within the grds (336/OTHER ATTRACTIONS). For café only, enter by Arboretum Pl. Catering-style food with light meals at lunch time, self-service; distinctly lacklustre. But o/side tables and the view of the city are everything. Also squirrels. 10am-5pm.

193
xE4

METROPOLE: 668 4999. 33 Newington Rd. Once a bank, now a civilised coffee house – the premises lend an air of Art Deco something. On a quiet afternoon it's where a Newington mum might mull over her life, the children at the nursery. Accompanied by a cappuccino with cinnamon . . . at least. 9am-10pm daily.

194
D3

THE LOWER AISLE: Underneath St Giles Cathedral (340/OTHER ATTRACTIONS), enter round back via Parliament Sq, or through the body o' the kirk. Proximity of courts sees many legal eagles swooping in, tourists who have this book and regulars for coffee, tea, light meals. Mon-Fri 9am-4.30pm, Sun 10am-2pm. Cl Sat.

195
D3

CAFFE SARDI: 220 5553. 18-20 Forrest Rd. More a restau perhaps with all the expected dishes but also serves a mean Danish pastry and espresso. Coffee machine is a Big Gold Dream and with waitresses from the old country and Italian television on cable, a hint of Soho's Bar Italia. Mon-Sat 9.30am-11pm, Sun 3-11pm.

196
B2

ROUND THE WORLD: 15 NW Circus Pl, Stockbridge. Exceptional gift shop and kitchenware vendor with startling coffee bar in converted bank (once mine). Tea, cake and one of the v best espressos. Open 10am-6pm Mon-Sat.

197
C4

LA GRANDE CAFETIERE: 228 1188. 182-184 Bruntsfield Pl. Coffee shop during the day, popular bistro at night (INX). In among assorted coffees and herbal teas, Bovril can be had. Nice restful alternative to brash Montpeliers opp (81/CHAINS-U-LIKE). 9am-11pm, until 12midnight Thu-Sat. 10am-6pm Sun.

198
E4, D3

CALIFORNIA COFFEE CO: 228 5001. By the Odeon cinema (Clerk St), top of Middle Meadow Walk (opp Forrest Rd). 7.45am-9pm Mon-Fri, 10am-9pm Sat-Sun. Hope Park Cres, 8.30am-7pm Mon-Fri, 10am-7pm Sat-Sun. Caffeine kiosks in former police boxes. Similar fare to Seattle (*see above*). Plans afoot for others.

GREAT CAFÉS AND GREASY SPOONS

✝ BLUE MOON CAFÉ: 557 0911. 36 Broughton St. Longest-established gay café in the capital and still evolving (412/GAY EDIN). Now houses an espresso bar as well as the main bit with breakfast, snacks, meals or a drink. Female staff efficient, boys more spacey. Free condoms in the gents for the impecunious or impatient. 7am-12midnight Sun-Thu, 7am-1am Fri-Sat. LO 40mins before close.

199
D2

NDEBELE: 221 1141. 59 Home St, Tollcross. The Ndebele are a southern African people, but this café has dishes from all over the continent so get your ostrich, mielie bread and biltong shavings here – or just have a coffee. Does loads of sandwiches, light meals and has a good groovalong soundtrack. Africa distant and usually hot, this delightfully chilled. Daily 10am-10pm.

200
C4

CENTRAL CAFÉ: 228 8550. 42 Home St, next to the Cameo Cinema. Graham Main's downtown deli/takeaway with urban cool and gr snacks and coffee (no cooking). Best music and crack in the area, esp Faye, their famous waitress (on Sat only). 8am-6pm. Cl Sun.

201
C4

LE MENU: 467 7847. 248 Dalry Rd. An oasis in the Gorgie lands – a small but superior café by day selling snacks and meals, transforms into a down-home French bistro at night (BYOB). Dead cheap and pretty good fun. Mon-Sat 8.30am-9.30pm, shuts for an hr at tea time to effect its transformation.

202
A4

CAFFE EUROPA: 667 6116. 53 Clerk St. Formerly Wayfarers, now a much more Italian-style establishment but still quite cheap. If you don't want the *pesce al forno*, there's always the Europa Mixed Grill – absolutely everything your medical adviser told you never to eat on one plate for a few quid. 10am-8pm daily.

203
A4

CANASTA: 554 5190. 10 Bonnington Rd, nr corner with Gr Jnct St, Leith. Café for locals, not one of your downtown cappuccino numbers. Best omelettes in the burg, and usual café grub (haddock and chips, grills) and cakes home-made before you (I) get up. Tea in a mug. Takeaway. We should honour these people. Cl Sun.

204
xD1

KUDOS: 558 1270. 2 Greenside Pl, next to Playhouse. Gay café-bar with light meal/snack menu. 12noon-1am daily, LO food 8pm.

205
D2

KEBAB MAHAL: 667 5214. Nicolson Sq. Cult I. Report: 149/INDIAN.

KUSHI'S: 556 8996. 16 Drummond St. Cult II. Report: 150/INDIAN.

INTERNET CAFÉS

206
C2

CYBERIA: 220 4403. 88 Hanover St. If we can split hairs and say there's a distinction between cool and hip, then Cyberia takes the silicon wafer for coolest capital Internet café. Good coffee, fine sandwiches and cakes – you'd come for an espresso even if you had no interest in cyberspace. E-mail drop box facility, surfing sessions by the half hr, etc. V chic, understated décor with sculpturey bits. E-mail: edinburgh@cybersurf.co.uk. Mon-Sat 10am-10pm, Sun 12noon-7pm. Staff most likely to say: 'Hi! And what can I getcha?' in fetching Antipodean accent.

207
C3

WEB 13: 229 8883. 13 Bread St. The city's most homely Internet boutique. At quieter times, bloke who looks much more attuned to messing around with motherboards will muck in to make you a sandwich. Again, all the usual facs for web, e-mail, etc. Quarter- and half-hr rates, dozen PCs, colour scanning, printing and all that jazz. E-mail: queries@web13.co.uk. Had a place in our researcher's heart as virtual home of the Aber FC e-mail list. Mon-Fri 9am-8pm, Sat 9am-6pm, Sun 11am-5pm. Staff most likely to say: 'Guy here wants to know about a Shockwave plug-in for Netscape 5.0 beta.'

THE BEST CUPS OF COFFEE

208
D3

CAFFE SARDI: 220 5553. 18-20 Forrest Rd. Quietly Italian, quietly fab, the coffee machine is a wonder in itself and, by Giorgio, they make a damn fine espresso.

209
C2

ROUND THE WORLD: 225 7800. 15 NW Circus Pl. My old bank! Now a styly gift shop with a very chic coffee bar and classic machine.

210
C2

SEATTLE COFFEE COMPANY: 226 3610. 128 Princes St. American-influenced concession with phenomenal range of coffee-based drinks. (187/BEST TEAROOMS)

211
D3

MAISON HECTOR: 332 5328. 47 Deanhaugh St, Stockbridge. Creamy cappuccino comes with a Flake – nice touch. Talking of cappuccino, **BROUGHTON ST BRASSERIE** (558 5355, 2 Broughton Pl) does a fluffy cup. Fluffy staff too.

212
D3

FRUITMARKET CAFÉ: 226 1843. 29 Market St. Best art gallery coffee (although **STILLS** in Cockburn St is a contender).

When out and about, try a **CALIFORNIA COFFEE COMPANY** booth. Details on all above, see BEST TEAROOMS and SUNDAY BREAKFAST.

THE BEST LATE-NIGHT RESTAURANTS

✝ ✝ **BLUE:** 221 1222. Cambridge St. Upstairs in the Traverse Theatre building. The café-bar associated with the Atrium (55/BEST RESTAUS), so the food's pretty good and you can graze and snack until 12midnight (same menu all day) in the place to be seen. (66/BEST BISTROS)   INX

213
C3

✝ **WITCHERY:** 225 5613. Castlehill, top of Royal Mile nr the Castle. Not open v late, but does take bookings up until 11.30pm, that crucial half hr beyond 11 that allows you to eat after the movies. Special after-theatre menu from 10.30pm has 2 courses for under £10, a v good deal from one of the best restaus in town. 7 days, lunch and LO 11.30pm. (57/BEST RESTAUS)   MED

214
C3

✝ **INDIGO YARD:** 220 5603. 7 Charlotte Lane. Late supper menu till 1am in fashionable, throbbing set of rms (with similar clientele). Seductive menu, but loud. Report: 69/BEST BISTROS.

215
B3

✝ **NICOLSON'S:** 557 4567. 6a Nicolson St, upstairs opp Festival Theatre. Convenient and v Edin kind of bistro until 12midnight (LO 11.30pm). Diverse menu; late-night people. (74/BISTROS)

216
D3

THE BLUE MOON CAFÉ: 556 2788. 36 Broughton St. Gay café-bar in the quarter. Burgers to bagels. Go on, they won't bite you (or maybe they will). LO 11.20pm (12.20am Fri-Sat). (199/CAFÉS)

217
D2

GORDON'S TRATTORIA: 225 7992. 231 High St. Although some tired and emotional late-night visitors mistake this for a kebab house, it's v definitely Italian. Pasta 'n' pizza 'n' fish until the sma' hrs. Sun-Thurs 12noon-12midnight, Fri-Sat 12noon-3am.   INX

218
D3

BAR ROMA: 226 2977. 39a Queensferry St. 2mins from the Caledonian Hotel at the W End of Princes St; busy day and night. Big rm with a real buzz attracts all sorts from late owls to families for Sunday lunch. Basic pizza, pasta but smarter than your av wine list. 12noon-12midnight Sun-Thu; until 3am Fri-Sat.   INX

219
B3

PEPE'S TAVERNA: 337 9774. 96 Dalry Rd. Here's one to know about; good and friendly and open until 2.30am (though cl Tue). (101/ITALIAN RESTAUS)   CHP

220
A4

ESSO SERVICE STATION: Canonmills. All-night pitstop of choice.

221
A4

SAINSBURY'S, BLACKHALL: Fri night 24hrs; cruising the aisles.

222
xA2

GOOD PLACES FOR SUNDAY BREAKFAST

223
D3

✝ **CAFÉ FLORENTIN:** St Giles St, off Royal Mile opp Cathedral. The first to open for a civilised start (or finish). The authentically French coffee shop with croissants/pain au chocolat and the best whirly pastries in town. May be too early to eat cake. From 7am. (183/BEST TEAROOMS)

224
C4

✝ **KAFFE POLITIK:** 446 9873. 146-148 Marchmont Rd. Quite possibly the best scrambled eggs with emmental and chives on toast in town. And good coffee in serenely cerebral surroundings. From 10am. (185/BEST TEAROOMS)

225
B1

MAISON HECTOR: Raeburn Pl. Eggs Benedict, Finnan haddies, Toulouse sausage, smoked salmon omelette or yer full-on fry-up in designery surroundings courtesy of Alloa Breweries. Sun papers provided (79/BEST BISTROS). Brunch 11am-4pm.

226
C3

IGUANA: 220 4288. 41 Lothian St. Even the appearance of a bizarre lentil croquette thing in the middle of the all-day vegn breakfast wasn't enough to stir the cynicism of our researcher. Service uploaded by blue-bloused femmes wearing Destiny Angel headsets in this café-bar with self-proclaimed cool (295/THESE ARE HIP). From 9am daily.

227
C3

NEGOCIANTS: 45-47 Lothian St. Nr univ. Gr all-round pub (THESE ARE HIP), open v late and v early on Sunday for breakfast. From 9am (brunch till 6pm). May be tables o/side.

228
D2

SMOKE STACK: 556 6032. 53-55 Broughton St. In Maison Hector's league as far as Sun brunch is concerned – Arbroath smokies, Eggs Florentine or Benedict, all-out brekkers, vegn or carnivore style in burgundy and blue diner (169/BURGERS). 12noon-4pm.

229
D2, D1

THE BROUGHTON ST BREAKFAST: Meanwhile, elsewhere in Edin's hippest st, the upsurge of café-bar culture offers many good bets for brekkers. From the top down: **THE CATWALK** opens at 10am for both veggies and carnivores, while **BAROQUE** kicks in from 12.30pm with similar nosh (slightly more exp). Round the corner in Broughton St Lane, **THE OUTHOUSE** opens at 12.30pm and serves a more elaborate brunch menu through to 4pm (see THESE ARE HIP for details of all 3). For a pubbier experience, try the **BARONY** further down the st (242/GREAT EDIN PUBS). Cheap, cheerful, papers to peruse.

THE BEST TAKEAWAY PLACES

✚ **ROWLAND'S:** 225 3711. 42 Howe St. Top-notch New Town takeaway with hot dishes that change daily (never predictable, e.g. Sri Lankan chicken curry). Interesting sandwich rolls, excellent cheeses, bread, cakes and other carefully selected fare. Also does o/side catering (mmm . . . those Thai prawns) and you can phone your order. Mon-Fri 8am-5pm. Cl Sat-Sun.

230
C2

✚ **GLASS & THOMPSON:** 557 0909. 2 Dundas St. Deli and coffee shop on main st in New Town, but also takeaway sandwiches/rolls in infinite formats using their drool-making selection of quality ingredients (breads, cheeses, salamis, etc). Ready-made Mediterranean snacks like wood-cooked aubergines, pâtés, tortes. Take away to office, grds or dinner party. Excellent sit-in area and small terr for whiling away Edin days. Mon-Fri 8.30am-6.30pm, Sat 8.30am-5.30pm, Sun 11am-4.30pm. (191/BEST TEAROOMS)

231
C2

✚ **BUTLER'S:** 229 7737. Lady Lawson St. Our office often make the detour over to Butler's at the top of the Grassmarket. Imaginative sandwiches and gr hot dishes not lost by microwaving. Good vegn burger, cakes and pies. Cl Sat-Sun.

232
C3

THE GLOBE: 558 3837. 42 Broughton St. A bright spot on the corner in the middle of Edin's coolest st; this place is one of the reasons why. Open all day until 4/5pm for sandwiches/rolls and toasted focaccia. Big window for people watching. Cl Sun.

233
D2

EASTERN SPICES: 558 3609. 2 Canonmills Br, by the clock. On the grapevine, this place is better than most – phone in your order or turn up and wait. Also home delivery. Full Indian menu from pakora to pasanda and vegn meals for one – if you're down at the end of lonely st.

234
C1

CAPPUCCINO EXPRESS: 622 7447. 62 Cockburn St. Some tables o/side in summer and a few stools inside; an Italian takeaway *par excellence*. Soup, pasta and fab ciabatta/focaccia sandwiches with excellent fillings in olive oil. Mon-Sat 8am-6pm. Cl Sun.

235
D3

CHARLIE McNAIR'S: 226 6434. 30 Forrest Rd. Best on the S side. Fab sandwiches. Mon-Fri 9am-5.45pm, Sat 9.30am-4pm. Cl Sun.

236
D3

THE FORREST: 225 4560. 52 George IV Br. Nr libraries and Edin Univ. Long-time fave of ours. Mon-Fri 6.30am-3pm. Cl Sat-Sun.

237
D3

SALVATORE'S: 228 2334. 6 Gillespie Pl, Bruntsfield. Stonking Italian takeaway. 10am-11pm daily.

238
C4

VALVONA & CROLLA 'the legendary deli' (page 40)

WHERE TO DRINK

SOME GREAT 'EDINBURGH' PUBS

239
xE1

☩ ☩ **PORT O' LEITH:** 58 Constitution St. You could walk into this bar once every 5yrs and be hard pushed to see any changes. Occasionally wild, usually interesting, always a gr leveller. The distilled spirit of auld Leith untouched by business/service developments in the last decade; no place for snobs. Good soundtrack both verbal and musical. Until 12.45am daily.

240
D2

☩ **CAFÉ ROYAL:** Behind Burger King at the E end of Princes St, one of Edin's longest celebrated pubs. Unrelated to the London version, though there is a similar Victorian/Baroque elegance. Through the partition is the Oyster Bar (117/SEAFOOD RESTAUS). Central counter and often standing rm only. If you're going out on the tiles, the tiles here are a good place to start. Mon-Wed 11am-11pm, Thu to 12midnight, Fri-Sat to 1am, Sun 12.30pm-11pm.

241
xC4

☩ **BENNET'S:** Leven St, by King's Theatre. Just stand at the back and watch light stream through the stained glass on a sunny day. Same era as Café Royal and similar ambience, mirrors and tiles. Decent food at lunch (285/PUB FOOD). Until 11.30pm Mon-Wed, 12.30am Thu-Sat, 11pm Sun.

242
D1

BARONY BAR: 81 Broughton St. Real-ale venue with a young profile and occasional live music; also some Belgian and wheat beers. Newspapers on hand to browse over a Sun afternoon breakfast or a (big) lunch time pie. Until 12 midnight Mon-Thu, 12.30am Fri-Sat, 11pm Sun.

243
D2, C2
B3, xE1

THE OYSTER BARS: Calton Rd (St James), 16a Queen St (Queen St); 28 W Maitland St (W End); 10 Burgess St, The Shore (Leith). All mentioned elsewhere but also here because, though the Brothers Donkin (whose empire they comprise) are Geordies, the Oyster Bars are a pure Edin creation. First two are most typical for ambience and good music (313/LIVE MUSIC).

244
D3

EL BAR: 558 9139. 15 Blackfriars St. It looks like a rm that used to be something else with a few second-hand tables scattered around. It's small and it sells tapas, bocatas, Cruzcampo and plato del dia. Really scruffy, really Spanish and really good; we love it even when they run out of wine. Until 1am daily.

THE BASEMENT: 109 Broughton St. Now much-imitated, which must count as flattery, this is a chunky, happening sort of, er, basement where you can have Mex-style food during the day served by laaarvely staff in Hawaiian shirts. At night, the punters are well up for it – late, loud and lively. Until 1am daily.

245
D2

BAR KOHL: 54 George IV Br. Nr libraries and univ. A dedicated vodka bar – first in Europe – ideal if you want to get off your face drinking rare Siberian spirit with all the young dudes, but good anyway. Avoid sillier flavours like bubble gum. Cool Keith Haringesque toilets. Until 1am daily.

246
D3

SHEEP'S HEID: 656 6952. The Causeway, Duddingston Village. Not central, but a pleasant and dramatic drive away behind Arthur's Seat in the Queen's Park. Old coaching inn with good crack, some locals, patio gdn and decent grub (283/PUB FOOD). Food until 9pm, pub 11pm (12midnight Fri-Sat).

247
xE4

KAY'S BAR: 39 Jamaica St. The New Town – incl Jamaica St – sometimes gives the impression that it's populated by people who were around in the late 18th century. Drop in here sometime and you'll see what we mean. The clothes may be contemporary, the vibe is anything but. And they care for their beer (269/REAL -ALE PUBS). Until 11.45pm (11pm Sun).

248
C2

MATHER'S: 1 Queensferry St. Edin's W End has a complement of 'smart' bars that cater to men with tight haircuts and women with tight mouths. The alternative is here – a stand-up space for old-fashioned pubbery, slack coiffure and idle talk (258/'UNSPOILT' PUBS). Until 12midnight Mon-Thu, 1am Fri-Sat, 11pm Sun.

249
B3

ROBBIE'S: Leith Walk, on corner with Iona St. Some bars on Leith Walk are downright scary – but not this one. Tolerant, good range of beer, TV will have the football on often as not. Wild mix of Trainspotters, locals and the odd dodgy character or three, even a stray social worker (HQ is nearby). But if all you want to do is read the paper, you'll be left well alone (255/'UNSPOILT' PUBS). Until 12midnight Mon-Sat, 11pm Sun.

250
E1

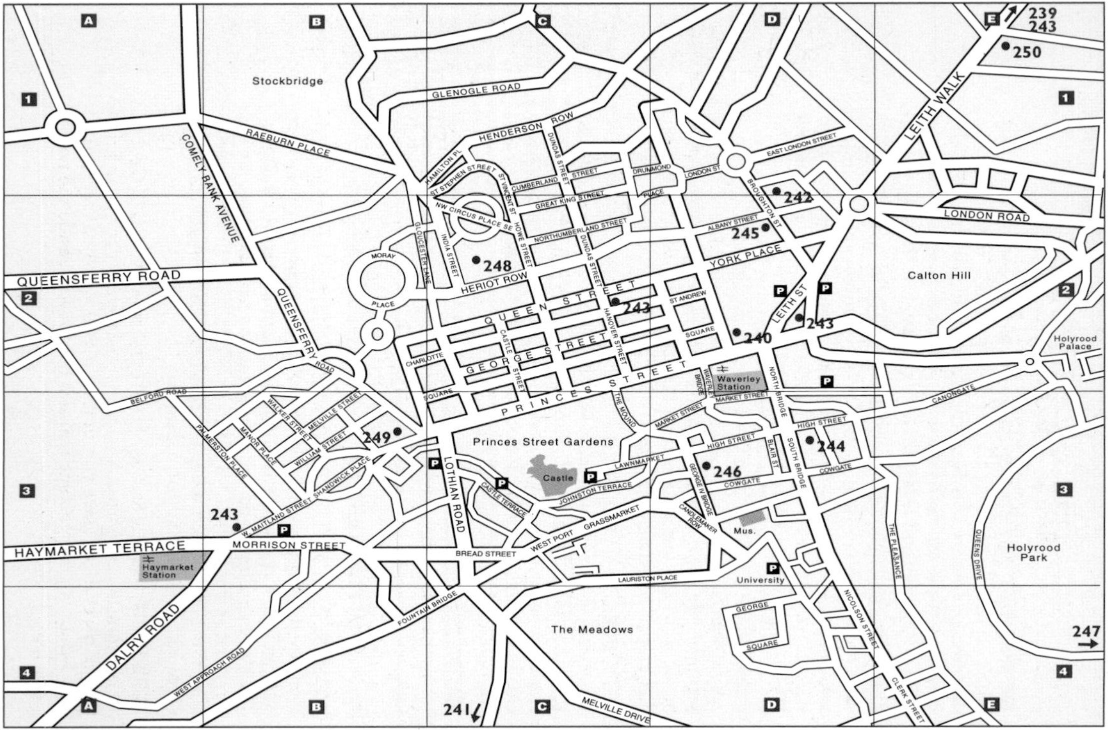

Map labels and features:

- Stockbridge
- Calton Hill
- Holyrood Park
- Princes Street Gardens
- Castle
- The Meadows
- Haymarket Station
- Waverley Station
- University
- Mus

Streets and roads:
- LEITH WALK
- LONDON ROAD
- QUEENSFERRY ROAD
- GLENOGLE ROAD
- RAEBURN PLACE
- COMELY BANK AVENUE
- QUEENSFERRY STREET
- HAYMARKET TERRACE
- DALRY ROAD
- MORRISON STREET
- LOTHIAN ROAD
- HENDERSON ROW
- DUNDAS STREET
- HANOVER STREET
- FREDERICK STREET
- CASTLE STREET
- CHARLOTTE STREET
- GEORGE STREET
- YORK PLACE
- BROUGHTON ST
- LEITH ST
- NORTH BRIDGE
- SOUTH BRIDGE
- BLAIR ST
- GEORGE IV BRIDGE
- THE MOUND
- PRINCES STREET
- THE PLEASANCE
- NICOLSON STREET
- CLERK STREET
- MELVILLE DRIVE
- QUEENS DRIVE
- WEST LOUISBURGH
- INDIA STREET
- HERIOT ROW
- GLOUCESTER LANE
- HOWE STREET
- ST VINCENT ST
- GREAT KING STREET
- DRUMMOND PLACE
- BREAD STREET
- WEST PORT
- LAURISTON PLACE
- GRASSMARKET
- CANDLEMAKER ROW
- MORAY PLACE
- QUEEN STREET
- THISTLE STREET
- ROSE STREET

Pub reference numbers:
- 1/239, 243, 250 (E1)
- 247 (D2)
- 245 (D)
- 240
- 243
- 244
- 246
- 243
- 248
- 249
- 243
- 247 (E4)
- 241

Grid references: 1, 2, 3, 4 (top and bottom); A, B, C, D, E (left and right)

THE BEST OLD 'UNSPOILT' PUBS

Of course it's not necessarily the case that when a pub's done up, it's spoiled, or that all old pubs are worth preserving, but some have resisted change and that's part of their appeal. Money and effort are often spent to 'oldify' bars and contrive an atmos. The following places don't have to try.

THE DIGGERS: 1 Angle Park Terr. (Officially the Athletic Arms.) Jambo pub *par excellence*, stowed with the Tynecastle faithful before and after games. Still keeps a gr pint of McEwan's 80/-, allegedly the best in Edin. The food is basic pies and stovies. Until 12midnight Mon-Sat, 6pm Sun.

251
A4

ROSEBURN BAR: 1 Roseburn Terr, on main Glas rd out W from Haymarket and one of the nearest pubs to Murrayfield Stadium. Wood and grandeur and red leather, bonny wee snug, fine pint of McEwan's and wall-to-wall rugby of course. Heaving before internationals. Until 11pm Sun-Wed, 12midnight Thu-Sat.

252
xA3

CLARK'S: 142 Dundas St. A couple of snug snugs, red leather, brewery mirrors and decidedly no frills. Good McEwan's – just the place to pop in if you're tooling downhill from town to Canonmills. A local you would learn to love. Until 11pm (11.30pm Thurs-Sat).

253
C1

BLUE BLAZER: 2 Spittal St. No frills, no pretensions just wooden fixtures and fittings, pies and toasties in this fine S&N-owned howf that usually carries half a dozen real ales. More soul than any of its competitors nearby. Mon-Thurs 11am-12midnight, Fri-Sat 11am-12.30am, Sun 12.30pm-11pm.

254
C3

ROBBIE'S: Leith Walk, on corner with Iona St. Real ales a-go-go in a smoky old neighbourhood howf that tolerates everyone from the wifie in her raincoat to multi-pierced yoof of indeterminate gender. More rough than smooth of course, but with the footy on the box, pint of Bass, packet of Hula Hoops – this bar can save your life. Irvine Welsh wuz here, and me. Until 12midnight Mon-Sat, 11pm Sun. (250/GREAT EDIN PUBS)

255
xE1

OXFORD BAR: 8 Young St, one of the lanes behind W end of George St. No time machine needed – just step in the door to see an Edin that hasn't changed since yon times. Careful what you say; this is an off-duty cop shop. Some real ales but they're beside the point. Until 1am (12midnight Sun).

256
C2

257
C3

FIDDLER'S ARMS: 9 Grassmarket. On a corner at the W end of the Grassmarket and about the only pub in the area that hasn't been interfered with, except for a relatively new carpet. Has McEwan's 80/-, real fiddlers Mon nights. A pre-theme bar. Until 12midnight (1am Fri-Sat).

258
B2

MATHER'S: 1 Queensferry St. Not only a reasonable real-ale pub but almost worth visiting just to look at the ornate fixtures and fittings – frieze and bar esp. The latter looks as if it was carefully hewn from a single lump of wood by a Stakhanovite Victorian – they don't make 'em like that these days. Unreconstructed in every sense. Until 12midnight Mon-Thu, 1am Fri-Sat, 11pm Sun. (249/GREAT EDIN PUBS) There's another, unrelated, **MATHER'S** in Broughton St which is managing to keep its head above water in the city's grooviest thoroughfare by remaining pub-like and unpretentious.

259
D3

STEWART'S: 14 Drummond St on the S side and just off S Br. Lino, beer, pensioners and folk who sing when in their cups. Few concessions to anything that has happened to the licensed trade since the 1960s. Until 12midnight Mon-Sat, 11pm Sun.

260
D3

THE ROYAL OAK: Infirmary St. Tiny upstairs and not much bigger down. During the day, pensioners sip their pints (couple of real ales) while the cellar until 2am.

261
D2

THE CENTRAL BAR: 7 Leith Walk. Once grand and still echoes its past, but now perhaps anachronistic. Tiled walls, ornate ceiling, green leather seats, cheap beer. It's been said before – if this was at the top of Leith Walk it would be yuppie paradise . . . but it's not. Worth a look though. Until 11pm daily.

262
C4

INTERNATIONAL BAR: 15 Brougham Pl, Tollcross. A sprinkling of real ales in this locals' howf – some students given its location. No frills, but until 1am daily.

THE BEST REAL-ALE PUBS

Pubs on other pages may have or feature real ale, but the following are the ones where they take it seriously and/or have a good choice.

THE CUMBERLAND BAR: Cumberland St, corner of Dundonald St. After work this New Town bar attracts its share of irritating mobile phone addicts – but later the locals reclaim it and Camra (Campaign for Real Ale) supporters seek it out too. Average of 12 real ales on tap. Nicely appointed, decent pub lunches, unexpected beer grd. Mon-Wed until 11.30pm, Thu-Sat to 12midnight. Sun opening in summer, may be extended.

263
C1

STARBANK INN: 64 Laverockbank Rd, Newhaven. On the seafront rd W of Newhaven harbour. Usually 9 different ales on offer. Gr place to sit with pint in hand and watch the sun sink over the Forth. Also does food. Bar until 11pm Sun-Wed, 12midnight Thu-Sat.

264
xC1

THE BOW BAR: 80 W Bow, halfway down Victoria St. They know how to treat drink in this excellent wee bar. Ask for a whisky – a fair few available – and there's no insane rigmarole about ice in the glass. Laphraoig, for example, comes straight as nature intended. Bliss. There are real ales you won't find anywhere else in the city. Until 11.30pm Mon-Sat, 11pm Sun.

265
D3

THE GUILDFORD ARMS: 1 W Register St. Behind Burger King at E end of Princes St (opp Balmoral Hotel) on same block as the Café Royal (240/GREAT EDIN PUBS). Lofty, ornate Victorian hostelry with loadsa good ales. Pub grub available on 'gallery' floor as well as bar. Sun-Wed until 11pm, Thu-Sat until 12midnight.

266
D2

BERT'S: 29 William St. Rare ales, a suit and twinset crowd after work but a fair mix at other times in this faux Victorian bar. Decent pies for carnivores or veggies alike and a good place to escape from uptown neurosis. Until 11pm Sun-Thu, 12midnight Fri-Sat. More local **BERT'S** at 2 Raeburn Pl, Stockbridge.

267
B3, B1

THE CANNY MAN: 237 Morningside Rd. Officially known as the Volunteer Arms, but everybody calls it the Canny Man. Good smorrebrod at lunch time (278/PUB FOOD), and wide range of real ales. Casual visitors may feel that management have an attitude (problem).

268
xC4

KAY'S BAR: 39 Jamaica St, off India St in the New Town. Go on an afternoon when gentlemen of a certain age talk politics, history

269
B7

and football over pints of real ale. The bow-tied barman patiently serves. All red and black and vaguely distinguished with a tiny snug – The Library. Until 11.45pm (11pm Sun). (247/GREAT EDIN PUBS)

270
D2

CASK & BARREL: 115 Broughton St. Wall-to-wall distressed wood, gr selection of real ales and the only bar in Edin where they've realised that samosas make ideal snacks. Also does pub grub, sometimes Thai-flavoured. Until 12.30am Sun-Wed, 1am Thu-Sat.

271
C4

CLOISTERS: 26 Brougham St, Tollcross. Nine real ales on tap in this simple and unfussy bar with its wooden panelling and laid-back app. Same owners as Bow Bar (*see above*). Basic pub grub at lunch times, bar closes 12midnight (12.30am Fri-Sat).

272
A4

CALEY SAMPLE ROOM: 5-8 Angle Park Terr. Half-owned by the nearby (independent) Caledonian Brewery, the CSR sells all the expected Caledonian real ales and a couple of guests besides. A neighbourhood bar most of the time, a haven for home and away fans before and after games at Tynecastle. Basic pub lunches Mon-Fri, drink served until 12midnight Sun-Thu, 1am Fri-Sat.

273
xE1

THE MERMAN: 42 Bernard St, Leith. Formerly Tod's Tap and hasn't changed much. Good range of real ales, real fire in the big rm through the back. Real pub really. Promotes itself as an antidote to orange and blue hip bar fatigue. Until 11pm (12midnight Fri-Sat).

274
xE4, D3,
C3

FIRKINS: Physician & Firkin, 58 Dalkeith Rd; Footlights & Firkin, 7 Spittal St; Fling & Firkin, 49 Rose St. Coming to us courtesy of Alloa – so not an independent chain. But they brew their own at Dalkeith Rd and supply all the local Firkins. Formula pubs – wood, food and real ales from light Summer Swallow to mental Dogbolter. F*rk*n jokes wearing thin. Generally until 1am daily.

275

CALEDONIAN BEER FESTIVAL: An annual event held around the first w/end in June at Edin's own – and independent – Caledonian Brewery, a red-brick Victorian pile at 42 Slateford Rd (on rt-hand side going out of town). It's a gr site, 50 real ales from Adnams to Whitbread on tap, food and music (esp jazz) on Thu-Sat evenings and Sun afternoon in the brewery's own 'Festival Hall', a refurbed bottling plant. See local press for details or call 337 1286. The 'Festival Hall' also hosts ceilidhs every Sat. (405/CEILIDHS)

PUBS WITH GOOD FOOD

✠ **THE SHORE:** 553 5080. 3 The Shore. A bistro/restau but the
same (blackboard) menu faster and friendlier in the bar (where
you can smoke). Light meat dishes, lots of fish and always something vegn. Lunch and LO 10pm. (71/BEST BISTROS)

276
xE1

✠ **KING'S WARK:** 554 9260. 36 The Shore, on the corner of
Bernard St. Woody, candlelit, absolutely fine. A business
haunt at lunch times and a good informal restau-cum-bar in the
evenings. Scottish slant on the menu, incl excellent fish in beer bat-
ter and chips; also food at the bar and real ales. Lunch and LO
10pm. Bar open to 11pm, 12midnight Fri-Sat.

277
xE1

✠ **THE CANNY MAN:** 447 1484. 237 Morningside Rd (aka The
Volunteer Arms) on the A702 via Tollcross, 7km from centre.
Idiosyncratic renowned eaterie with a certain hauteur. Carries a
complement of malts as long as a gr big long thing, serious wine
list and excellent smorrebrod lunch attack (12noon-3pm daily). B-
listed building with monkey-jacketed bar staff, cigars for sale – a
shrine to the good life. No loonies or undesirables welcome (you
may be tested). Until 12midnight Mon-Sat, 11pm Sun. (268/REAL-
ALE PUBS)

278
xC4

BLACK BO'S: 557 6136. 57 Blackfriars St. Adj to vegn restau of same
name (121/VEGN RESTAUS), the bar offers good coffee, snacks and
meals during the day with the restau taking over in the evening.
Where to go for vegn haggis filos with rosemary and green ginger
sauce. DJs at night. 11am-1am daily.

279
D3

CELLAR NO. 1: 225 7183. 1a Chambers St. Former bistro now
knocking out a fine standard of bar food with a Med twist from its
subterranean premises. Lunch and LO 10pm Mon-Sat, no food
Sun. Thu is flamenco night; Wed, Fri, Sat live jazz. Bar Mon-Thu
12noon-1am, Fri-Sat 12noon-3am, Sun 6pm-1am. Same people
have opened new bistro on corner of Chambers St/S Br (downstairs v much preferred).

280
D3

OLD CHAIN PIER: 552 1233. 1 Trinity Cres, on the Forth just W of
Newhaven Harbour. Rt on the waterfront, off the beaten track.
Been here for yrs but now considerably smarter than it was – still
v approachable with friendly staff. Well-kept real ale, gr bar snacks
(stilton with oatcakes, interesting toasties) and excellent-value bar
meals. LO food 8pm (but ask nicely after 8 and you never know).
Bar 12noon-11pm Sun-Wed, until 12midnight Thu-Sat.

281
xD1

282
C2

DRUM AND MONKEY: 538 8111. 80 Queen St. Clubby, city suit kind of bar with odd lady taking coffee in the pm. Smarter than your average pub grub with occasional Mediterranean influences and Scottish faves. Jazz on Sat afternoons, food until 10pm, couple of real ales. Bar 11am-12midnight Mon-Thu, until 1am Fri-Sat.

283
xE4

SHEEP'S HEID: 656 6952. Causeway, Duddingston Village. An 18th-century coaching inn 10km from centre behind Arthur's Seat and reached most easily through the Queen's Park. Restau upstairs and decent pub food down, incl alfresco dining in summer. The village and the nearby wildfowl loch should be strolled around if you have time. Food until 9pm incl Sun.

284
C4

THE GOLF TAVERN: 229 3235. 31 Wright's Houses. Off Bruntsfield Pl facing on to the links. V English country pub style with hearty food (beef 'n' ale pie, sausage and mash), couple of Chesterfields for slumping purposes; clientele can be a bit XR3i. LO food 7.30pm. Bar closes 12midnight daily.

285
C4

BENNET'S: 229 5143. 8 Leven St, next to the King's Theatre. An Edin standby, it could be listed for several reasons (241/GREAT EDIN PUBS), not least for its honest-to-goodness (and cheap) pub lunch. À la carte (sausage, fish, steak pie, etc) and daily specials under the enormous mirrors. Lunch only, 12noon-2pm.

286
D2

THE ABBOTSFORD: 225 5276. 3 Rose St. A doughty remnant of Rose St drinking days of yore, and still the best pub lunch nr Princes St. Nothing fancy in the à la carte of grills and mainly meaty entrées. Huge portions. LO in bar 3pm. Restau upstairs serves food in evening too – LO 9.45pm. Bar until 11pm. Cl Sun.

287
C2

THE DOME: 624 8624. 14 George St. Terribly big. Former bank and grandiose in the way that only a converted temple to Mammon could be. Main part sits 15m under elegant domed roof with island bar and raised platform at back for determined diners. Staff almost impeccable, pricey menu; you come for the surroundings more than the victuals (MED). Lunch 12noon-6pm, LO dinner 10pm daily. Also snack menu for casual diners away from roped-off posh nosh area. Adj real-ale bar Frazers is separate, more intimate, better for the tête-à-tête (or blether). Final bit, downstairs: *Why not?* a nightclub for over-25s: well, let us count the ways . . . Main bar Sun-Thu until 11.30pm, Fri-Sat until 1am.

OUTSIDE TOWN

THE SUN INN, LOTHIANBURN: 663 2456. On a bend of the A7 nr
t/off for Newtongrange, under mega viaduct, 18km S of city centre. Happy, homely pub in the unfashionable netherlands of
Midlothian. Bistro-style food, lunch and LO 9.30pm. Always a
couple of real ales – one from the Broughton Brewery.

288
xE4

THE BRIDGE INN / THE POP INN, RATHO, W LOTHIAN: 333 1320. 16km
W of centre via A71, turning rt opp Dalmahoy Golf Club. Large
choice of comforting food in canalside setting. Has won various
awards, incl accolades for its kids' menu. Restau, bar food and
canal cruises with nosh. Pop Inn 12noon-9pm daily. Restau lunch
daily and LO 9pm Mon-Sat. Bar until 11pm, 12midnight Fri-Sat.
(176/KID-FRIENDLY)

289
xA4

DROVER'S INN, EAST LINTON: 01620 860298. 5 Bridge St. Off the
A1, 35km S of city. Fair way to go for eats, but don't think about
the A1, think about the food, much improved of late. A classic village pub with warmth and delicious meals in bistro beside bar or
restau up top. Beer grd out back is o/looked and trains whoosh by,
but on a sunny day, partake their excellent lunch here. Lunch and
dinner (6-9.30pm) daily.

290
xE2

THESE ARE HIP

291
C2

PO-NA-NA: 226 2224. 43b Frederick St. A case of souk it and see in this popular N African theme bar – part of a chain but not obtrusively. Functions as a bar until 11pm, then it's more of a club with entry charge and DJs, and maybe a queue to get in. 7 days until 3am. The fag machine is covered in zebra skin. Fun.

292
D2

THE OUTHOUSE: 557 6668. 12a Broughton St Lane. Not an avowedly gay establishment, but happily mixed of an evening when there's a nice atmos in this v contemporary café-bar. Modish food available 12noon-4pm for self-conscious business diners and a regular Sun barbecue on the patio (not the greatest of views though). A Portishead remix kind of place. Until 1am.

293
B3

INDIGO YARD: 220 5603. 7 Charlotte Lane, off Queensferry St. Tucked away in the W End, this spacious designer café-bar (numero uno 1997) offers exposed brickwork, balcony tables, booths and babes in blue of both genders serving good food and drink. More Med than Mex cuisine with flexible menu, but possibly too loud later on for serious dining (69/BEST BISTROS). Until 1am daily. Same people have **IGUANA** (*see below*) and **MONTPELIERS** (81/CHAINS-U-LIKE).

294
C3

TRAVERSE THEATRE BAR: Downstairs at the Traverse Theatre, Cambridge St (387/NIGHTLIFE). One of the first Edin bars to go in for designer furniture, rolling art exhibs and all that jazz. Still trendy if a bit arch. Food 10am-8pm if no show, until 10pm when there's something on. Gr buzz pre- and post-performance. Bar until 12midnight Sun, Tue, Wed; 11pm Mon; 1am Fri-Sat. Much later during Festival when it's one of the nerve centres. Good place to meet nice people.

295
C3

IGUANA: 220 4288. 41 Lothian St. From the makers of Montpeliers (81/CHAINS-U-LIKE) comes this self-consciously clubby café-bar over the road from Edin Univ's Bristo Sq buildings – so v studenty in term time. DJs (Thu-Sat) play ambient/dub/dance later on. During the day people eat, drink or sip coffee in calm, cool surroundings (by Glasgow's Graven Images). Good all-day veggie breakfast, LO food 8.30pm. 9am-1am daily. (226/SUNDAY BREAKFAST, 319/LIVE MUSIC)

296
D3

NEGOCIANTS: 225 6313. 45-47 Lothian St. (Pron 'Nigoshunts' by locals.) Mirrors, food, space and shooters (non-lethal variety) upstairs; dancefloor, DJs (every night), drink and more drink down. Range of clients from civilised bagel-nibblers mid-morning to Chimayed-out dance fiends in the wee small hours. Zanier and less pretentious than Iguana next door, claim the waitresses – but just as studenty. Table service lacks pace – but hey! LO food 2.30am. Open 9am-3am daily.

SIRIUS: 555 3344. 7-10 Dock Pl, Leith. 'Designed' without being dreadful – quite harmonious really and almost democratic in the clientele mix it attracts. Gr energy about the place on the night-out nights, cocktail pitchers abound – wet Wed afternoon muzak would be *Wonderwall*. Does coffee and food in that eclectic, flexible style (i.e. Med-Mex). Until 12midnight Sun-Wed, 1am Thu-Sat.

297
xE1

THE WATER SHED: 220 3774. 44 St Stephen St. Neighbourhood café-bar with *de rigueur* light wood, blue and orange décor. Coffee/food served 10am-7pm (yes, Med-Mex inevitably), really kicks in as a bar later on – open until 1am daily. Share a cocktail or some cheap Chardonnay with Stockbridge's shiny happy people.

298

BAROQUE: Broughton St. Once more into the breach for Med-Mex. Décor-wise, the designer was presumably given a few monographs on Matisse, some on Gaudí, a lot of drugs and told to do something extravagant. The result is the most orange and blue bar in Edin but potty enough to be appealing. Our design consultant said: 'Why have recessed low-voltage lights then turn them up bright?' Who cares? Not here . . . LO food 7pm, bar until 1am daily.

299
D2

THE CATWALK CAFÉ: 478 7770. 2 Picardy Pl on the 'Playhouse R/bout' at top of Broughton St. Concrete grey – maybe the new blue 'n' orange. Who knows because this latest addition to 'hip bars in Edin' gets mixed reviews, but is mobbed at w/ends. Two levels, a catwalk. Food until 6pm, downstairs DJ. A design departure in the city, its future seems assured; at least until the next time. We shall see.

300
D2

THE BEST PLACES TO DRINK OUTDOORS

301
xE1

THE SHORE: 553 5080. 3 The Shore, Leith. Excellent place to eat (71/BEST BISTROS), some tables just o/side the door, but it's fine to wander over to the dock on the other side of the st and sit with your legs over the edge. Do try not to fall in. From 11am daily.

302
xE1

THE WATERFRONT: 554 7427. 1c Dock Pl. Another v good Leith eaterie (70/BEST BISTROS) but with waterside tables and adj barge for those who fancy a float. Gr wine list. From 12noon Mon-Sat, 12.30pm Sun.

303
D4

PEAR TREE: 667 7533. 38 W Nicholson St. Adj to parts of Edin Univ so real student-style with biggest beer grd in the capital and refectory-style food. From 11am Mon-Sat, 12.30pm Sun.

304
D2

THE OUTHOUSE: 557 6668. 12a Broughton St Lane. Large patio out back, home to summer Sun afternoon barbecues. (Not a gr view unfortunately.) (292/THESE ARE HIP)

305
D3

THE GREEN TREE: 225 1294. 180-184 Cowgate. Like a concrete plaza in a peripheral housing scheme – but 2mins from Royal Mile and somewhere to sit out of the traffic. From 12noon daily.

306

General locations: try **GREENSIDE PL** (**THEATRE ROYAL** and **KUDOS**), bars in **THE GRASSMARKET**, and **IGUANA** and **NEGOCIANTS** (295/296/THESE ARE HIP) on **LOTHIAN ST**. All make a stab at pavement café culture when the sun's out.

THE BEST IRISH BARS

Authentic links to the old country or just the big breweries promulgating a bunch of Erse? Irish bars have emerged in a big way in Edin as everywhere else in the last couple of yrs. Only time will tell if they'll last. For the moment, the best are:

FIBBER McGHEE'S: 220 2376. 24 Howe St. The city's smartest, shiniest Irish bar without doubt (New Town location of course). Breakfast and bar food 7 days, LO 6pm, live Irish folk music most Sats. The portrait of Joyce is a nice touch. Until 1am daily.

307
C2

FINNEGAN'S WAKE: 226 3816. 9b Victoria St. Giving this bar its due, you'll hear appropriate accents among the clientele. Solid-sent cavern hung with all kind of knick-knacks from over the Irish Sea. A place for drink and music, then more drink. Folk sessions around 10pm every night. Until 1am daily.

308
C2

BIDDY MULLIGAN'S: 220 1246. 96 Grassmarket. Good-time bar in the heart of w/end drinking country with adj Thistle Inn (28/ECONOMY HOTELS). Live music some nights; bar food, coffee and breakfast all day until 8pm; drink is taken until 1am daily. Staff are as Irish as the average Australian ('G'day!', etc).

309
C3

O'NEILL'S: 225 4680. 99 Hanover St. Tennents' excursion into ersatz Oirishness and with a haberdashery theme (don't ask) one that can ping the bogosity meter. But v fab staff, the bar menu makes concessions to Irish food (potato pancakes) and there's music 3 nights a week (1 folk sesh, 2 nights with wannabe Bonos) so gets lively. Until 12midnight Sun-Thu, 1am Fri-Sat. The other 'branch' of **O'NEILL'S** at S Br has a hardware theme.

310
C2

FINN MacCOOL'S: Lothian Rd. Now this is what we call an Irish pub. Flavoured vodkas, big-screen MTV, drinks promos for students, cheesy dance music in the background – as Irish as the 1994 World Cup team. Pool table downstairs. Until 1am Mon-Sat, 12midnight Sun.

311
C3

THE GOOD LIVE MUSIC

312
D3

✠ **TRON CEILIDH HOUSE:** 226 0931. 9 Hunter Sq, behind Tron Kirk. Three levels. Bar on ground floor with folk jam Sat-Sun afternoons; labyrinth at basement 1 with similar folk jam sesh Sun-Thu evenings; basement 2 has comedy club, songwriters night and more folk. Gr real ales. Sun-Thu to 12midnight, Fri-Sat to 1am.

313
D2, C2
xE1, B3

THE OYSTER BARS: ST JAMES: 557 2925. Calton Rd, opp St James Centre and off the top of Leith Walk. Live music Wed night. Food daily, LO 10pm. More music at **QUEEN ST OYSTER BAR** (basement oncorner of Queen St and Hanover St). Wee bands Mon, Tue and Thu (226 2530). Other Oyster Bars at **THE SHORE** (Leith) and **WEST END** (W Maitland St). All open until 1am. (243/GREAT EDIN PUBS)

314
D2

THE VENUE: 557 3073. Calton Rd, behind Waverley Stn. Edin's major live venue at club level with well-established dance clubs at w/ends like Pure and Tribal Funktion. For live music, it's on the UK club circuit, so often notable bands and the best of the Scottish wannabes. Watch for posters and flyers. (401/ROCK AND POP)

315
D3

LA BELLE ANGELE: 225 2774. 11 Hasties Close, behind the Kitchen and the Living Room in the Cowgate (323/325/LATE BARS). Combines its role as a DJ club and live music venue well. Rm has attitude and atmos. (401/ROCK AND POP)

316
C3

THE CAS ROCK: 229 4341. 104 W Port. Nr art college. Musical oasis in Edin's pubic triangle, the area full of bars with 'dancers'. No-nonsense, Indie/alternative thrashing in small space. Hot, sweaty, beery rock 'n' roll. Until 1am daily.

317
D3

THE LIQUID ROOM: 225 2564. At the top of Victoria St. Recent face-lift. Enter at st level and descend to watch bands before they go on to greater things (or not). For details consult *The List*. Times vary. Also a major club venue for clubs called Evol and Liquid.

318
D3, C3

SUBWAY: 225 6766. Cowgate, under George IV Br. Cavernous grungey rock 'n' roll. Fairly studenty, live music some nights, DJs on others playing 1960s to cheesy dance. 5pm-3am daily. Also **SUBWAY WEST END,** 23 Lothian Rd. Glitzier than its Cowgate cousin. Nothing live; DJs playing Indie, 1970s, 1980s.

319
D3

NEGOCIANTS: 225 6313. 45 Lothian St. Basement DJs in bar for young dudes. Upstairs café-bar serving interesting food; bustling with studentish crowd, LO food 2.30am. 9am-3am daily. **IGUANA** next door also does cool tunes. Reports: 295/296/THESE ARE HIP.

THE BEST LATE BARS

NEGOCIANTS: 45 Lothian St, by Univ Union buildings. Civilised café/ restau/bar upstairs and basement with DJs. Open until 3am every night. Full reports: 296/THESE ARE HIP, 319/LIVE MUSIC.

320
D3

PO-NA-NA: 43b Frederick St. More of a club than a bar later on perhaps but open to 3am daily. Think Morocco. Young crowd; queue at w/ends. (291/THESE ARE HIP)

321
C2

WHISTLEBINKIES: 4-6 S Br. Central drinking dungeon with live music 7 nights, until 3am. Distressed rock 'n' roll. No windows.

322
B3

THE LIVING ROOM: 235 Cowgate, adj The Kitchen (*see below*). A pavement with a roof, a balcony and some designer twiddles with its share of lassies in microfrocks and proto-Damons and Liams who may manage a club later, or may not. 7pm-3am daily. Pretty dead until 10-ish. Commercial dance 7 nights. Tense. (If you complain once more, you'll meet army of me. Bouncers that is . . .)

323
D3

THE ROYAL OAK: Infirmary St, nr the top and S Br. Run by ex-White Heather Club dancer Sandra Adams, this place is a folk institution. Locals drink in the tiny bar upstairs during the day, live sessions kick-off downstairs every night around 10pm with well-kent faces dropping in occasionally for the tunes and the singaround. Until 2am daily. (260/'UNSPOILT' PUBS)

324
D3

THE KITCHEN: 237 Cowgate. An ante-rm for the city's club scene, this is the place if you want a pint of 80/- before moving on. Taken over by S&N recently. DJs Thu-Sat play hip hop, house and disco/funk/soul – loadsa students. Pub grub until 7pm daily. Bar 11am-1am daily. V different to The Living Room (*see above*). 'We hate them,' said the barman.

325
D3

CC BLOOMS: Greenside Pl. Late-night gay venue with bar upstairs (catch the floorshow and eye contact generally) and downstairs dancefloor. Until 3am. (409/GAY EDIN)

326
D2

THE BOUNDARY BAR: 379 Leith Walk. Early rather than late – people really do turn up here at 5am for a drink because that's when it opens. Basic and unlovely old beer outlet on the old boundary betw Edin and Leith, and betw now and then. Does it really matter when it shuts?

327
E1

Not-so-very late bars (until 1am) include **IGUANA**, **INDIGO YARD**, **THE WATERSHED**, **BAROQUE** (all THESE ARE HIP) and the **OYSTER BARS** (243/GREAT EDIN PUBS).

IGUANA 'DJs later on' (page 78)

WHERE TO GO IN TOWN

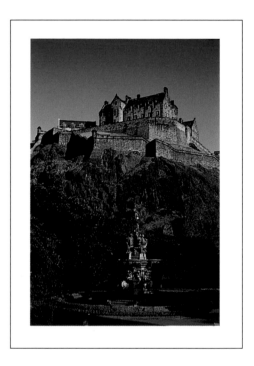

EDINBURGH CASTLE 'the main attraction' (page 87)

THE MAIN ATTRACTIONS

✝ ✝ ✝ **EDINBURGH CASTLE:** Go to Princes St and look up. The main attraction, extremely busy in summer. Tartan tea cosies on sale in the shop rake in the bawbees. And yet. St Margaret's 12th-century chapel is simple and beautiful, the rolling history lesson that leads up to the display of Scotland's crown jewels is fascinating; the newly installed Stone of Destiny is a big deal to the Scots (though others may not see why). And, ultimately, the Scottish National War Memorial is one of the most genuinely affecting places in the country – a simple, dignified testament to shared pain and loss. Last ticket 45mins before closing. Apr-Sep 9.30am-6pm, Oct-Mar 9.30am-5pm. HS

328
C3

✝ ✝ **HOLYROOD PALACE:** Foot of the Royal Mile. Queenie's N Brit time-share – she's here for a wee while at end June/beginning July every yr. Large parts of the palace are dull (Duke of Hamilton's loo, Queen's wardrobes) so only a dozen or so rms are open, most dating from 17th century but a couple from the earlier 16th-century bit. Lovely cornices abound. Anomalous Stuart features, adj 12th-century abbey ruins quite interesting. Upper-class shop, so get your souvenirs here. Apr-Oct: Mon-Sat 9.30am-5.15pm (last ticket), Sun 9.30am-4.30pm (last ticket). Nov-Mar: 9.30am-3.45pm (last ticket) daily. Now open New Year's Day. HS

329
E2

✝ ✝ **THE ROYAL MILE:** The High St, the medieval main thoroughfare of Edin following the trail from the volcanic crag of Castle Rock and connecting the 2 landmarks above. Heaving during the Festival but if on a winter's night you chance by with a frost settling on the cobbles and there's no one around, it's magical. Always interesting with its wynds and closes (Dunbar's Close, Whitehorse Close, the secret grd opp Huntly House), but lots of tacky tartan shops too. See it on a walking tour – there are several esp at night (ghost/ghouls/witches, etc). Some of the best actually take you under the st. Mercat Tours (661 4541) are pretty good. Also Robin's (661 0125) and Witchery (225 6745).

330
C3, D3,
E3, E4

✝ ✝ **ROYAL SCOTTISH MUSEUM:** Chambers St. From the big whale skeleton to archaeological artefacts, design exhibs to stuffed elephants, it's all here. Building designed by Captain Francis Fowkes, Royal Engineers, and completed in 1888. Ab fab atrium soars way up high. Huge new extension (with the story of Scotland) has ETA of St Andrew's Day 1998 and is tipped to be

331
D3

one of the most important new buildings of the decade. Mon-Sat 10am-5pm, Sun 12noon-5pm. ADMN

332
C2

✙ ✙ **NATIONAL GALLERY** and **ROYAL SCOTTISH ACADEMY:** The Mound. The National is the rear of the 2 Neoclassical buildings on Princes St and houses a superb collection of Old Masters in a series of hushed salons. Many are world famous, but you don't emerge goggle-eyed as you do from the National in London – more quietly elevated (FREE). The Playfair 'temple' on Princes St itself is the **RSA**; changing exhibs which in early summer and midwinter show work from contemporary Scottish artists (ADMN). Both galleries 10am-5pm, Sun 2-5pm.

333
xA3

✙ ✙ **EDINBURGH ZOO:** 334 9171. Corstorphine Rd. 4km W of Princes St, buses from Princes St Gdns side. Whatever you think of zoos, this one is highly respected and its serious zoology is still fun for kids (organised activities in Jul/Aug). The penguins waddle out at 2pm daily and the melancholy, accusing eyes of the wolves connect with onlookers in a profoundly disconcerting manner. Open AYR. Mon-Sat 9am-6pm, Sun 9.30am-6pm. (443/WHERE TO TAKE KIDS) ADMN

334
xE4

✙ ✙ **ROYAL COMMONWEALTH POOL:** 667 7211. Dalkeith Rd. Hugely successful pool complex which includes a 50m main pool, a gym, sauna/steam rm/suntan suites and a jungle of flumes. Goes like a fair, morning to night. Some people find the water overtreated and too noisy, but Edin has many good pools to choose from; this is the one that young folk prefer. Some lane swimming. Mon-Fri 9am-9pm, Sat-Sun 10am-4pm (7pm in summer).

335
xA2

✙ ✙ ✙ **THE FORTH BRIDGE:** S Queensferry, 20km W of Edin via A90. First turning for S Queensferry from dual carriageway; don't confuse with signs for road br. Or train from Waverley to Dalmeny, and walk 1km. Knocking on now and showing its age, the br was 100 in 1990. But still . . . Can't see too many private finance initiative wallahs rushing in to do anything of similar scope these days – who would have the vision? An international symbol of Scotland, it should be seen. How about from the N Queensferry side (well, I live at the S end)?

A B C D E

1 2 3 4

335 ← QUEENSFERRY ROAD

333 ← HAYMARKET TERRACE

Stockbridge

Comely Bank Avenue

Queensferry

Raeburn Place

Glenogle Road

Henderson Row

Dundas Street

St Vincent St

Howe Street

Heriot Row

India Street

Gloucester Lane

Murray Place

Leith Walk

Broughton St

York Place

London Road

Calton Hill

Holyrood Palace

329

Holyrood Park

Queens Drive

The Pleasance

Clerk Street

Nicolson Street

334

University

Mus **331**

George IV Bridge

Candlemaker Row

Chambers St

Lauriston Place

The Meadows

Melville Drive

Bread Street

West Port

Grassmarket

Castle

Princes Street Gardens

Lothian Road

Hanover Street

The Mound

Frederick Street

Castle Street

George Street

Charlotte Square

Queensferry Street

Princes Street

North Bridge

South Bridge

Blair St

Waverley Station

330

332

Morrison Street

Haymarket Station

Dalry Road

Haymarket Terrace

328

Leith St

THE OTHER ATTRACTIONS

336
B1

ROYAL BOTANIC GARDEN: 552 7171. Inverleith Row, 3km from Princes St. Bus nos 23, 27. Enter from Inverleith Row or Arboretum Pl. 70 acres of ornamental grds, trees and walkways; a joy in every season. Tropical plant houses, well-groomed rock and heath grd and enough space just to wander. New Chinese Grd coming on nicely, precocious squirrels everywhere. But don't jog – or they'll getcha. Gallery with occasional exhibs and café with outdoor terr for serene afternoon teas (192/BEST TEAROOMS). The natural high. Open 7 days 10am-4pm (Nov-Feb), 6pm (Mar-Apr/Sep-Oct) and 8pm (May-Aug).

337
D2

NATIONAL PORTRAIT GALLERY: 556 8921. 1 Queen St. Sir Robert Rowand Anderson's fabulous and custom-built neo-Gothic pile houses paintings and photos of the good, gr and merely famous. Danny McGrain hangs out next to the Queen Mum and Nasmyth's familiar pic of Burns is here. Good venue for photo exhibs, beautiful atrium with star-flecked ceiling and frieze of (mainly) men in Scottish history from a Stone-Age chiel to Carlyle. Splendid. Gr café (182/BEST TEAROOMS). Mon-Sat 10am-5pm, Sun 2-5pm.

338
xA2

GALLERY OF MODERN ART: 556 8921. Belford Rd. Betw Queensferry Rd and Dean Village (nice to walk through). Best to start from Palmerston Pl and keep left. Former school with permanent collection from Impressionism to Hockney and the Scottish painters alongside. An intimate space where you can fall in love with paintings on winter afternoons. Important temporary exhibs. The café is excellent (180/BEST TEAROOMS). Mon-Sat 10am-5pm, Sun 2-5pm.

339
D3

MUSEUM OF CHILDHOOD: 200 2000. 42 High St. Local authority-run shrine to the dreamstuff of tender days where you'll find everything from tin soldiers to Lady Penelope on video. Full of adults saying, 'I had one of them!' Child-size mannequins in upper gallery can foment an *Avengers*-era spookiness if you're up there alone. Mon-Sat 10am-5pm. Cl Sun. (444/WHERE TO TAKE KIDS)

340
D3

ST GILES' CATHEDRAL: Royal Mile. Not a cathedral really, although it was once – the High Kirk of Edin, Church of Scotland central and heart of the city since the 9th century. The building is mainly medieval with Norman fragments and all encased in a Georgian exterior. Lorimer's oddly ornate Thistle chapel and the 'big new organ' are impressive. Simple, austere design and bronze of John Knox set the tone historically. Holy Communion daily and other regular services. Good coffee shop in the crypt (194/BEST TEAROOMS). Summer: Mon-Fri 9am-7pm, Sat 9am-5pm, Sun 1-5pm. Winter: Mon-Sat 9am-5pm, Sun 1-5pm.

THE GEORGIAN HOUSE: 225 2160. 7 Charlotte Sq. Built in the 1790s, this town house is full of period furniture and fittings. Not many rms, but the dining-rm and kitchen are drop-dead gorgeous – you want to eat and cook there. Delightful ladies from the National Trust for Scotland answer your queries. Moderator of the General Assembly of the Church of Scotland bides up the stair. Apr-Oct 10am-5pm, Sun 2-5pm. Last admn 4.30pm.

341
B2

NTS

LAURISTON CASTLE: 336 2060. 2 Cramond Rd S. 9km W of centre by A90, turning rt for Cramond. Elegant architecture and gracious living from Edwardian times. A largely Jacobean tower house set in tranquil grounds o/looking the Forth. The liveability of the house and the preoccupations of the Reid family make you wish you could poke around for yourself, but there are valuable and exquisite decorative pieces and furniture and it's guided tours only. You could always continue to Cramond for the air (344/WALKS IN THE CITY). Apr-Oct 11am-5pm (cl lunch, cl Fri); Nov-Mar 2-4pm, w/ends only.

342
xA2

ADMN

BUTTERFLY FARM, NR DALKEITH: Report: 445/WHERE TO TAKE KIDS.

DEEP SEA WORLD, NORTH QUEENSFERRY: Report: 446/WHERE TO TAKE KIDS.

ARTHUR'S SEAT: Report: 343/WALKS IN THE CITY.

THE PENTLANDS: Report: 428/WALKS OUTSIDE THE CITY.

THE SCOTT MONUMENT/CALTON HILL: Report: 347/349/BEST VIEWS.

THE BEST WALKS IN THE CITY

See page 10 for walk codes.

343
E3

ARTHUR'S SEAT: Of many walks, a good circular one taking in the wilder bits, the lochs and gr views (348/BEST VIEWS) starts from St Margaret's Loch at the far end of the park from Holyrood Palace. Leaving the car park, skirt the loch and head for the ruined chapel. Pass it on your rt and, after 250m in a dry valley, the buttress of the main summit rears above you on the rt. Keeping it to the rt, ascend over a saddle joining the main route from Dunsapie Loch which appears below on the left. Crow Hill is the other peak crowned by a triangular cairn – both can be slippery when wet. From Arthur's Seat head for and traverse the long steep incline of Salisbury Crags. Paths parallel to the edge lead back to the chapel. (Incidentally, nae mt bikes off tarmac or Sgt Sobotnicki will have words.)

START: Enter park at palace at foot of the High St and turn left on main road for 1km; the loch is on the rt.

PARK: There are car parks beside the loch and in front of the palace (paths start here too, across the rd).

5-8KM   CIRC   MT BIKE (RESTRICTED ACCESS)   2-B-2

344
xA2

CRAMOND: This is the charming village (not the suburb) on the Forth at the mouth of the Almond with a variety of gr walks. **(A)** To the rt along the 'prom'; the trad seaside stroll. **(B)** Across the causeway at low tide to Cramond Island (1km). Best to follow the tide out; this allows 4hrs (tides are posted). People have been known to stay the night in summer, but this is discouraged. **(C)** Cross the mouth of the Almond in the tiny passenger boat which comes on demand (summer 9am-7pm, winter 10am-4pm) then follow coastal path to Dalmeny House which is open to the public in the afternoons (May-Sept, Sun-Thu); or walk all the way to S Queensferry (8km). **(D)** Past the boathouse and up the R Almond Heritage Trail which goes eventually to the Cramond Brig Hotel on the A90 and thence to the old airport (3-8km). Though it goes through suburbs and seems to be on the flight path of the London shuttle, the Almond is a real river with a charm and ecosystem of its own. The Cramond Bistro (312 6555) on the riverside is not a bad wee bistro and awaits your return. BYOB. Cl Mon.

START: Leave centre by Queensferry Rd (A90), then rt following signs for Cramond. Cramond Rd N leads to Cramond Glebe Rd; go to end.

PARK: Large car park off Cramond Glebe Rd to rt. Walk 100m to sea.

1/3/8KM   XCIRC   BIKE   BUS 41   1-A-1

CORSTORPHINE HILL: W of centre, a knobbly hilly area of birch, beech and oak, criss-crossed by trails. A perfect place for the contemplation of life's little mysteries and mistakes. Or walking the dog. It has a radio mast, a ruined tower, a boundary with the wild plains of Africa (at the zoo) and a vast redundant nuclear shelter that nobody's supposed to know about. See how many you can spot. If it had a tearoom in an old pavilion, it would be perfect.

345
xA2

START: Leave centre by Queensferry Rd and 8km out turn left at lights, signed Clermiston. The hill is on your left for the next 2km.

PARK: Park where safe, on or nr this rd (Clermiston Rd).

1-7KM   CIRC   XBIKE   BUS 26, 85   1-A-1

WATER OF LEITH: The indefatigable wee river that runs from the Pentlands through the city and into the docks at Leith can be walked for most of its length, though obviously not by any circular route. (**A**) The longest section from Balerno 12km o/side the city, through Colinton Dell to the Tickled Trout pub car park on Lanark Rd (4km from city centre). The 'Dell' itself is a popular glen walk (1-2km).

346
D2

START: A70 to Currie, Juniper Green, Balerno; park by High School. (**B**) Dean Village to Stockbridge: enter through a marked gate opp Hilton Hotel on Belford Rd (combine with a visit to Gallery of Modern Art). (**C**) Warriston, through the spooky old graveyard, to The Shore in Leith (plenty of pubs to repair to). Enter by going to the end of the cul-de-sac at Warriston Cres in Canonmills; climb up the bank and turn left. Most of the Water of Leith Walkway (A, B and C) is cinder track.

8KM (OR LESS)   XCIRC   BIKE   BUS 43,44   1-A-1

THE BEST VIEWS OF THE CITY

347
E2

✚ ✚ **CALTON HILL:** Gr view of the city easily gained by walking up from E end of Princes St by Waterloo Pl, to the end of the buildings and then up stairs on the left. The City Observatory and the Greek-style folly lend an elegant backdrop to a panorama (unfolding as you walk round) where the view up Princes St and the sweep of the Forth estuary are particularly fine. At night, the city twinkles. Popular cruising area for gays – but can be dangerous. Destination of the Torchlight Procession on 29 Dec (part of Edin Hogmanay celebrations) with gr firework finale.

348
E3

✚ ✚ **ARTHUR'S SEAT:** W of city centre. Best app through Queen's Park from foot of Canongate by Holyrood Palace. The igneous core of an extinct volcano with the precipitous sill of Salisbury Crags presiding over the city and offering fine views for the fit. Top is 251m; on a clear day you can see 100km. Surprisingly wild considering proximity to city. (343/WALKS IN THE CITY)

349
D2

SCOTT MONUMENT: Princes St. Design inspiration for Thunderbird 3. This 1844 Gothic memorial to one of Scotland's best-kent literary sons rises 61.5m above the main drag and provides scope for the vertiginous to come to terms with their affliction. 287 steps mean it's no cakewalk; narrow stairwells weed out claustrophobics too. Those who make it to the top are rewarded with fine views. Underneath, a statue of the mournful Sir Walter gazes across at Jenners. Apr-Sep 9am-6pm; Oct-Mar 9am-3pm. Cl Sun. ADMN

350
C3

CAMERA OBSCURA: Castlehill, Royal Mile. At v top of st nr castle entrance, a tourist attraction that, surprisingly, has been there for over a century. You ascend through a shop, photography exhibs and holograms to the viewing area where a continuous stream of small groups are shown the effect of the giant revolving periscope thingie. All Edin life is visible – amazing how much fun can be had from a pin-hole camera with a focal length of 8.6m. Apr-Oct 9.30am-6pm, sometimes later. Nov-Mar 10am-5pm. ADMN

351
LOTHIANS
D1

NORTH BERWICK LAW: The conical volcanic hill, a beacon in the E Lothian landscape. **TRAPRAIN LAW** nearby is higher, tends to be frequented by rock-climbers, but has major prehistoric hillfort citadel of the Goddodin and a definite aura. BOTH 1-A-1

THE PENTLANDS/HERMITAGE: Reports: 428/427/WALKS O/SIDE CITY.

CASTLE RAMPARTS: Report: 328/MAIN ATTRACTIONS.

THE BEST SPORTS FACILITIES

SWIMMING AND INDOOR SPORTS CENTRES

ROYAL COMMONWEALTH POOL: 667 7211. Dalkeith Rd (334/MAIN ATTRACTIONS). The biggest, but Edin has many others. Recommended are **WARRENDER** (447 0052), Thirlestane Rd 500m beyond the Meadows S of centre; **LEITH VICTORIA** (555 4728), in Jnct Pl off the main st in Leith, now refurb with Pulse centre; **GLENOGLE** (343 6376) in Stockbridge, the New Town choice, v friendly. All these pools are old and tiled, 25yd long, seldom crowded and excellent for lane swimming – at certain times. All tend to have different sessions, so phone to check.

352
E4, xE3, xE1, C1

PORTOBELLO: Portobello Esplanade (441/BEACHES). Similar to others – closed for extensive refurb at time of writing but planning to reopen in 1998. Splendid Turkish baths have gone apparently – shame. Phone Royal Commonwealth Pool (*see above*) for info.

353
xE1

AINSLIE PARK: 551 2400. Pilton Dr off Ferry Rd, N of centre, 5km from Princes St; and **LEITH WATERWORLD:** 555 6000. Foot of Leith Walk. Leisure centres with water thrills for kids. Ainslie also has serious keep-fit side – lane swimming, gym, sauna, footie.

354
xC1, xE1

MEADOWBANK: 661 5351. London Rd. City athletics stadium with courts for squash and badminton (often booked), Pulse centre, weights room, 13m indoor climbing wall, outdoor football/hockey pitches and velodrome. No pool.

355
xE2

MARCO'S: 228 2141. 51 Grove St. Labyrinthine commercial centre with aerobic classes, gym, squash and snooker. No pool. Little Marco's will look after your kids while you sweat.

356
B3

UNIVERSITY GYM: 650 2585. The Pleasance. No-nonsense complex, v cheap. The best in town for weights (all the right machinery) and circuit training. Squash, badminton, indoor tennis, etc. Quiet in vacs, membership not required. For a reasonable fee, the Fitness and Sports Injury Centre (FASIC) is an excellent alternative to the 'take 2 aspirin and go away' school of GP. Few fake suntans.

357
E3

EDINBURGH CLUB: 556 8845. 2 Hillside Cres. Probably the most civilised of non hotel-type clubs. Usually members only, longer-stay visitors may be able to negotiate a rate. Good weights (mainly Universal), sauna/steam/sun/bistro. Good aerobics classes. And spinning, apparently. No pool.

358
E1

359
B3

DRUMSHEUGH BATHS CLUB: 225 2200. 5 Belford Rd, W End. Private swimming club in elegant building above Dean Village that costs a fortune to join and has an 18-month waiting list (so nae chance readers). But gorgeous Victorian pool with rings and trapeze over the water, sauna, multigym and bar. Frequented by the quality. If you're chums with a law lord, get him to sign you in as a guest.

GOLF COURSES

There are several municipal courses (see phone directory under City of Edin Council) and nearby, esp down the coast, some famous names that aren't open to nonmembers. Refer to Lothians map on pages 116–17.

360
xC4

BRAID HILLS: 447 6666. Braid Hills app. 2 18-hole courses (no. 2 summer only). Thought to be the best in town. Never boring; exhilarating views. Booking usually not essential, except w/ends. Women welcome (and that ain't true everywhere round here).

361
D1

GULLANE NO. 1: 01620 842255. The best of 3 courses around this pretty, twee village (35km down the coast) that was built for golf. Now you are really golfing! (though not on Sat).

362
D1

GLEN GOLF CLUB (aka NORTH BERWICK EAST): 01620 895288. Some say W is best (01620 892135) but most say E and few would argue that N Berwick on a fair day was worth the drive (36km, A1 then A198) from Edin. That's the Bass Rock out there, and Fidra. Open to women.

363
C1

MUSSELBURGH: The original home of golf (really: golf recorded here in 1672), but this local authority-run 9-hole links is not exactly top turf and is enclosed by Musselburgh Racecourse. Nostalgia still appeals though. **ROYAL MUSSELBURGH** nearby compensates. It dates to 1774, the fifth-oldest in Scotland. Busy early mornings and Fri afternoons, 01875 801139.

364
D2

GIFFORD: 01620 810267. Dinky inland course on the edge of a dinky village, bypassed by the queue for the big E Lothian courses and a guarded secret among the regulars. (Can't play after 4pm Tues/Wed/Sat or Sun afternoons.) 9 and 11 holes.

OTHER ACTIVITIES

365

TENNIS: There are lots of private clubs though only the **GRANGE** (332 2148) has lawn tennis and you won't get on there easily. There are places you can slip on (best not to talk about that), but the municipal centres (Edin residents/longer-stay visitors should get a Leisure Access card [661 5351] allowing advance reservation) are:

SAUGHTON: 444 0422. Stevenson Dr. 8km W of city centre. 2 astro-turf courts and one other. Also used for football, so phone to book.

366
xA4

CRAIGLOCKHART: 444 1969. Colinton Rd. 8km SW of centre via Morningside and Colinton Rd. 6 indoor courts, 7 outdoor and a 'centre court' – best to check/book by phone. Other separate sports facs incl squash, badminton and gym, 443 0101. Centre open Mon-Fri 9am-11pm, Sat-Sun 9am-10.30pm.

367
xC4

SKIING: Artificial slopes at **HILLEND** on A702, 10km S of centre. 445 4433. Excellent fac with various runs. The matting can be bloody rough when you fall and the chairlift is a bit of a dread for beginners, but once you can ski here, St Anton is all yours. Tuition every evening (not Thu) and w/ends. Open until 10pm in winter, 9pm in summer. Snowboarders have a plastic mountain.

368
xC4

PONY-TREKKING: LASSWADE RIDING SCHOOL: 663 7676. Lasswade exit from city bypass then A768, rt to Loanhead 1km and left to end of Kevock Rd. Full hacking and trekking facs and courses for all standards and ages.

369
D4

PENTLAND HILLS TREKKING CENTRE: 01968 661095. At Carlops on A702 (25km from town) has sturdy, steady Icelandic horses who will bear you good-naturedly into the hills. Exhilarating stuff. Bus from St Andrew's Sq.

370
xA4

ICE-SKATING: MURRAYFIELD ICERINK: 337 6933. Riversdale Cres, just off main Glas Rd nr zoo. Cheap, cheerful and chilly. It has been here forever and feels like a gr 1950s B movie ... go round! Sessions daily from 2.30pm.

371
xA3

ALIEN ROCK: 552 7211. Old St Andrew's Church, Pier Pl, Newhaven. Indoor rock climbing in a converted kirk. Laid back atmos, bouldering rm and interesting 12m walls of various gnarliness to scoot up. Daily; phone for sessions. Have a pint after in **THE STARBANK** or **THE OLD CHAIN PIER** nearby (281/PUB FOOD).

372
xD1

FORECORT LEISURE: 555 4533. Ashley Pl, off Newhaven Rd (opp Comet). Keith says we have to put this in as it's his local and he's a sucker for watching MTV while on the treadmill. 5-a-side football pitch, multigym, fitness studios, kids' play area and basic café.

373
xD1

THE BEST GALLERIES

Apart from those mentioned previously (MAIN ATTRACTIONS, OTHER ATTRACTIONS), *the following are always worth a look. Check* The List *magazine (fortnightly) for details.*

374
D3

CITY ART CENTRE: 529 3993. Market St. Quite big. This is the place the populist blockbuster exhibs come to as well as excellent social/educational displays. Sensibly curated city asset. Convenient if uninspiring café.

375
D3

THE FRUITMARKET GALLERY: Across the rd in Market St, a smaller, more warehousey space for more contemporary collections, retrospectives, installations. Café (181/BEST TEAROOMS) highly recommended for meeting and eating, watching the world go by.

376
D3

THE COLLECTIVE GALLERY: 220 1260. 22 Cockburn St. Innovative venue specialising in installations of Scottish and other young contemporary trailblazers. Members' work won't break the bank.

377
C2

THE SCOTTISH GALLERY: 558 1200. 16 Dundas St. Guy Peploe's influential New Town gallery on 2 floors. Where to go to buy something painted, sculpted, thrown or crafted by up-and-comers or established names – everything from affordable jewellery to original Joan Eardleys at £10k plus. Or just look.

378
C1

OPEN EYE GALLERY: 557 1020. 75-79 Cumberland St. Excellent small private gallery in residential part of New Town. Always worth checking out for accessible contemporary painting and ceramics. Almost too accessible (take cheque book).

379
D1

THE PRINTMAKERS' WORKSHOP AND GALLERY: 557 2479. 23 Union St, off Leith Walk nr London Rd r/bout. Workshops that you can look over. Exhibs of work by contemporary printmakers and shop where prints from many of the notable names in Scotland are on sale at reasonable prices. Bit of a treasure.

380
D1

BELLVUE GALLERY: 557 1663. 4 Bellvue Cres. Edin's newest small gallery at the bottom of fashionable Broughton St. Selected contemporary work in light salons (gallery is part of a house). The one to watch, the openings to go to. Afternoons.

381
D3

PHOTOGRAPHY: Edin is blessed with 2 contemporary photo-art venues. **STILLS:** 622 6200, 23 Cockburn St, recently closed for refurb, came back bolder, brighter in Oct 1997 with a café. **PORTFOLIO:** 220 1911, 43 Candlemaker Row, is a small 2-floor space in what used to be the city's left-wing bookshop.

GOOD NIGHTLIFE

For the current programmes of the places recommended below and all other venues, consult The List *magazine, on sale at most newsagents.*

MOVIES

Multiplex chains apart, these ones take movies seriously:

THE CAMEO: 228 4141. Home St in Tollcross. 3 screens showing important new films and cult classics. Some late movies at w/ends. Good bar.

382
C4

FILMHOUSE: 228 2688. Lothian Rd, opp Usher Hall. 3 screens with everything from first-run art-house movies to subtitled obscurities and retrospectives. Home of the annual Film Festival; café-bar (until 11.30pm Sun-Thu, 12.30am Fri-Sat) is a haven from the excesses of Lothian Rd. Open to non-cinephiles.

383
C3

THE DOMINION: 447 2660. Newbattle Terr, off Morningside Rd. Friendly, family-run cinema with 3 screens (one of them's like sitting in a plane). Nice wee place to see big films with the kids. Luca's ice cream.

384
xC4

THEATRE

The main city theatres are **THE FESTIVAL THEATRE:** 529 6000. Nicolson St. Edin's showcase theatre re-created from the old Empire with a huge glass frontage of bars and a stage and screen dock large enough to accommodate the world's major companies. Eclectic programme AYR.

385
D3

THE KING'S: 229 1201. Leven St, Tollcross. **THE LYCEUM:** 229 9697. Grindlay St. Ornate and lately refurb theatres with wide-ranging popular programmes.

386
C4

THE TRAVERSE: 228 1404. Small but influential, dedicated to new work (though mainly touring companies) in modern Euro, v architectural 2-theatre premises in Cambridge St (behind Lyceum). Good rendezvous bar in theatre (294/THESE ARE HIP) also excellent adj restau (55/BEST RESTAUS) and café-bar (66/BEST BISTROS).

387
C3

THEATRE WORKSHOP: 226 5425. 34 Hamilton Pl. A small neighbourhood theatre in Stockbridge with a wide reputation for vital, innovative work. Café-bar run by the Helios Fountain people (128/VEGN RESTAUS).

388
B1

389
C3, E4

CLASSICAL MUSIC

Usually from one of Scotland's national orchestras at regular concerts in the **USHER HALL** 228 1155. Lothian Rd. Smaller ensembles more occasionally at **THE REID, ST CECILIA'S** or **THE QUEEN'S HALL**. See *The List* or the Sat edition of the *Scotsman* newspaper.

JAZZ

390
C3

THE QUEEN'S HALL: 668 2019. Clerk St. Occasional 'concerts'; see press.

391

CELLAR No. 1: 225 7183. 1a Chambers St. Basement bistro and bar with light combos, where you will probably see all of Edin's best players at some time. Late. (280/PUB FOOD)

392
xE1

NOBLES: 554 2024. 44a Constitution St. Dependable bar food and real ales in a fine-sized rm. Folk on Thu, R&B Fri and jazz Sat, but phone to confirm. *xE1*

393

LEITH JAZZ FESTIVAL/ EDINBURGH JAZZ FESTIVAL: Late May/early Aug. Selected venues. Check *The List* for details or TO.

FOLK

See LIVE MUSIC. *Best bets on a regular basis are:*

394
D3

THE TRON CEILIDH HOUSE: 226 0931. Hunter Sq. One of Edin's major live venues, up and downstairs. Busy, friendly, folky.

395
D3

SANDY BELL'S aka **THE FORREST HILL BAR:** Forrest Hill. Famous and forever. Sometimes you could look in and wonder why; other times you know you're in exactly the rt place. Music every night except Tue and Sun.

396
D3

THE FIDDLER'S ARMS: Grassmarket. And fiddle they do on Mon nights. Good crack and blether at all times. (257/'UNSPOILT' PUBS)

397
B3

WEST END HOTEL: 225 3656. Palmerston Pl. A good place to stay or just to hang out with the Highlanders. Some trad folk live at w/ends and whenever. (21/INDIVIDUAL HOTELS)

398
D3

THE ROYAL OAK HALL: Infirmary St. Late-night singalong. (324/LATE BARS)

THE BEST ROCK AND POP MUSIC

PLAYHOUSE THEATRE: 557 2590. Greenside Pl. Major theatre in Scotland, most regular programme, holds 3,000. More infrequent as concert venue while they get through the musicals (not many to go).

399
D2

USHER HALL: 228 1155. Lothian Rd. Gr auditorium. Classier acts. Recent problems, so may be absent from current listings.

400
C3

THE VENUE: 557 3073 and **LA BELLE ANGELE:** 225 2774. Main small club venues for emerging and local bands. Check *The List* (fortnightly) for programmes. (314/315/LIVE MUSIC, 418/419/BEST CLUBS)

401
D2

QUEEN'S HALL: 668 2019. Clerk St. Most diverse (choral, jazz, art pop). Good atmos. Used every night; your best bet if you just want to go somewhere for decent music.

402
xE4

THE BEST CEILIDHS

THE ASSEMBLY ROOMS: 220 4349. George St. Municipal halls but grand, the venue for all kinds of culture (esp during the Festival), and though a long way from the draughty village hall kind of jig, they've been positively reeling to the sounds of the Robert Fish Band. Ceilidhs generally last Fri of the month. Watch local press, e.g. *The List* (fortnightly), for details and pay at the door.

403
C2

WEST END HOTEL: 225 3656. 35 Palmerston Pl. Edin's Heilan' hame hotel has occasional sessions of music/singing and storytelling (more like a trad ceilidh) but no dancing. This is where to come (or phone) to find out where the others are (occasional ceilidhs held in the church hall nearby). (21/INDIVIDUAL HOTELS)

404
B3

CALEDONIAN BREWERY: Contact: 01698 385251. Slateford Rd. At time of going to press, ceilidhs every Sat in the Festival Hall in the brewery 8-11.45pm. Bands vary but the couple of hundred heuchin' teuchin' punters have a good time regardless. (275/REAL-ALE PUBS)

405
A4

GAY EDINBURGH THE BEST!

Edin's gay scene continues to develop, though the 'pink triangle' around the Playhouse is now more of a circuit centred on Broughton St, where apart from the proclaimed gay bars, etc., there are now many gay-friendly places happy to cater for the 'community' and take the pink pound. As for other tourists, Edin is an easy city for the gay tourist to visit.

BARS AND CLUBS

406
D2
CAFÉ KUDOS: 556 4349. 22 Greenside Pl. Part of frontage of Playhouse Theatre. Civilised rather than overtly cruisy café-bar; epitomises Edin really. Now owned by a city councillor and a local radio stn DJ (where else in the UK would you get that?). Contemporary, light ambience with big open windows and tables in the st in summer. Food. You don't have to get drunk. 7 days until 1 am.

407
D2
NEW TOWN BAR: 538 7775. 26 Dublin St. Basement and v sub-basement bar in residential New Town. Mixed crowd. Island bar good for eyes across the rm. Downstairs – called **INTENSE**, open Thu-Sun – is fairly intense; cruisy and gets full-on. That carpet has seen everything. 7 days until 1.30am; w/ends 2.30am.

408
ROUTE 66: 557 3379. Few doors down from the Playhouse nr the next r/bout. Nothing special bar, but that's being picky. Major mid- to late-evening rendezvous and for those not necessarily … up for it. 7 days until 1am. You go there and then you go to:

409
D2
CC BLOOMS: 556 9331. Next to Playhouse. This is more like it (i.e. like every other Gay Bar UK); packed most nights upstairs and down (in the revamped disco). Last port of call for many, so gets Desperately Seeking Susan nr the dancefloor. Always queues nr the witching hr. After this there's only the 'Gardens of Fun' and that can be more risky than frisky, so get on with it here. 7 days until 3am. (326/LATE BARS)

410
C2
FRENCH CONNECTION: 225 7651. Rose St Lane N nr Castle St. Small, intimate bar out on a limb in the drinking zone. But that has its attractions. You will not come and go unnoticed. Oldies and youngies; the twain do meet. 7 days until 1am.

411
JOY: Info Line 467 2551. Scotland's 'most upfront' gay club gets moved about from pillar to post, but maybe that's how it keeps fresh 'n' wet. No point in a book that lasts 2yrs saying where they are now, but look out for flyers.

OTHER PLACES

BLUE MOON CAFÉ: 556 2788. 36 Broughton St. Friendly and always busy neighbourhood café at the heart of quarter with all-day menu and committed agenda. Non-gay friendly. 2/3 rms with food, drink and conversation. If you are arriving in Edin and don't know anybody, come here first. Food 7 days until 11.15pm, 12.15am w/ends. (199/CAFÉS)

412
D2

DSK: 478 7246. 32c Broughton St, nr the Blue Moon Café (*see above*). Prob pronounced 'dusk', a gay-friendly restau open at night (and Sun lunch). Cosmopolitan menu and outlook with more than a touch of Pacific Rim. Dinner before clubbing? Tue-Sun 7-10pm, Sun 12noon-3pm. MED

413
D2

NO. 18: 553 3222. 18 Albert Pl. Sauna for gentlemen. 12-10pm. Sun 2-10pm.

414
E1

HOTELS

MANSFIELD HOUSE: 556 7980. 57 Dublin St. Small New Town guest house and OK gay stay. Candelabra in the hall, various other camperie. Breakfast on a tray. No public rms – you'll have to leave your door open. New Town Bar (*see above*) up the st.

415
D2

5RMS   JAN-DEC   X/X   XPETS   XCC   XKIDS   MED.INX

LINDEN HOTEL: 557 4344. 9 Nelson St. Also in New Town. A real hotel; not exclusively gay. Thai restau (good) and bar. Prob the best for all-round facs, but not everyone here is a friend of Dorothy.   20RMS   JAN-DEC   T/T   PETS   CC   KIDS   INX

416
C2

GARLANDS: 554 4205. 48 Pilrig St. Quiet st of many other guest-houses about 2km from scene (but nr sauna).

417
xE1

5RMS   JAN-DEC   X/X   PETS   XCC   XKIDS   CHP

THE BEST CLUBS

Many of the best clubs come and go and there's little point in mentioning them here. Some are only on once a week with no permanent venue. Consult The List (fortnightly) for up-to-date info, and look for flyers. Edin club culture has improved a lot in the last 2 yrs. Most clubs are still weekly or occasional events, but they tend to use the same venues. Look out for:

418
D2

THE VENUE: 557 3073. Calton Rd, behind Waverley Stn. Long-established (in club terms) venue for clubs on w/end nights (mainly live bands during the week). Top nights – **PURE** (considered a major club night in Scotland), **TRIBAL FUNKTION**, **DISCO INFERNO** and **BOOGIE MO DYNAMO** (313/LIVE MUSIC)

419
D3

LA BELLE ANGELE: 225 2774. Hastie's Close, off Cowgate at Gilded Balloon. W/ends. Occupants vary but esp good fun are **YIP YAP**, **MANGA** and **BIG BEAT**. (315/LIVE MUSIC)

420
D3

CAVENDISH: 228 3252. W Tollcross, upstairs it has **THE MAMBO CLUB** Fri and Sat (on 2 floors) African/reggae/generally good vibes music for v mixed crowd – good for oldies who like to dance.

421
D3

MERCADO: 226 4224. 36-39 Market St, behind Waverley Stn. Probably Edin's longest-running club venue. Recent revamp and infusion of good club organizers means that it's a go-area again – try **TFIF** for fun or **BURGER QUEEN**.

422
D3

Two clubs that we hope hang around (but who knows?): soul jazz grooves at **LIZZARD LOUNGE** in **CAFÉ GRAFFITI** on Sat (Mansfield Pl Church, though venue moving at time of going to press) and **CLUB LATINO** which moves around, so look for flyers. Mix of all ages for live bands and home to the estimable **SALSA CELTICA**.

423
C2

THE DOME: 624 8633. George St. Home to **WHY NOT?**, a kind of disco-mating venue for over 25s.

424

GOING PLACES: Edin's trailblazing easy listening club. Long before it was hip they were playing airport and dinner-dance music here. Styly crowd of all ages. Venue changes, look for flyers or notices in Black Bo's, Blackfriars St (279/PUB FOOD).

425
D2

THE SHOOTING GALLERY: 557 1785. 32 Broughton St. Latest regular (w/ends) venue upstairs on 2 floors in hip quarter. Bright young things. The latest bright young things' thing.

426
E1

JOY: Scotland's best gay club. Has moved around in the last yr so check for flyers in The Blue Moon Café (412/GAY EDIN).

WHERE TO GO OUT OF TOWN

EASY WALKS OUTSIDE THE CITY

Buses mostly from St Andrew's Sq. Info: 225 3858. Refer to Lothians map on pages 116–17.

427
C2

HERMITAGE OF BRAID: Strictly speaking, this is still in town, but there's a real sense of being in a country glen and from the windy tops of the Braid Hills there are some marvellous views back over the city. Main track along the burn is easy to follow and you eventually come to Hermitage House info centre; any paths ascending to the rt take you to the ridge of Blackford Hill. In winter, there's a gr sledging place over the first br up to the left and across the main rd.

START: Blackford Glen Rd. Go S on Mayfield to main T-jnct with Liberton Rd, turn rt (signed Penicuik) then hard rt immediately.

1-4KM   CAN BE CIRC   XBIKE   BUS 7   1-A-1

428
B2

THE PENTLANDS: Alan Jackson, poet of this parish, once wrote: 'Look wifie, behind you, the wild Pentlands.' And wild they are – a serious range of hills rising to almost 600m, remote in parts and offering some fine walking. There are many paths up the various tops and round the lochs and reservoirs. (**A**) A good start in town is made by going off the bypass at Colinton, follow signs for Colinton Village, then the left fork up Woodhall Rd. Second left up Bonaly Rd (signed Bonaly Scout Camp). Drive/walk as far as you can (2km) and park by the gate leading to the hill proper where there is a map showing routes. The path to Glencorse is one of the classic Pentland walks. (**B**) Most walks start from signposted gateways on the A702 Biggar Rd. There are starts at Boghall (5km after Hillend ski slope); on the long straight stretch before Silverburn (a 10km path to Balerno); from Habbie's Howe about 18km from town; and from the village of Carlops, 22km from town. (**C**) The most popular start is probably from the visitor centre behind the Flotterstone Inn, also on the A702, 14km from town (decent pub lunch and 6-10pm, all day w/ends); trailboard and ranger service. The remoter tops around Loganlea reservoir are worth the extra mile.

1-20KM   CAN BE CIRC   MTBIKE   BUS 4 OR ST ANDR SQ   2-B-2

429
C2

ROSLIN GLEN: Special: spiritual, historical and enchanting, with a chapel, a ruined castle and woodland walks along the R Esk.

START: A701 from Mayfield or Newington (or bypass, t/off Penicuik, A702 then fork left on A703 to Roslin). Some parking at chapel (453/LOTHIANS), 500m from corner of Main St/Manse Rd, or follow B7003 to Rosewell (also marked Rosslynlee Hospital) and 1km from village the main car park is to the left.

1-8km XCIRC BIKE BUS ST ANDR SQ 1-A-1

ALMONDELL: A country park to W of city (18km) nr (and one of the best things about) Livingston. A deep, peaceful woody cleft with easy paths and riverine meadows. Fine for kids, lovers and dog walkers. Visitor centre with teashop. Trails marked.

430
B2

START: Best app from Edin by A71 via Sighthill. After Wilkieston, turn rt for Camp (B7015) then follow signs. Or A89 to Broxburn past start of M8. Follow signs from Broxburn.

2-8KM XCIRC BIKE BUS ST ANDR SQ 1-A-1

BEECRAIGS AND COCKLEROY HILL: Another country park SW of Linlithgow with trails and clearings in mixed woods, a deer farm and a fishing loch. Gr adventure playground for kids. Best is the climb and extraordinary view from Cockleroy Hill, far better than you'd expect for the effort. From Ben Lomond to the Bass Rock; and the gunge of Grangemouth in the sky to the E.

431
B1

START: M90 to Linlithgow (26km), through town and left on Preston Rd. Go on 4km, park is signed, but for hill you don't need to take the left turn. The hill, and nearest car park to it, are on the rt.

2-8KM CIRC MTBIKE BUS ST ANDR SQ 1-A-1

BORTHWICK AND CRICHTON CASTLES: Takes in 2 impressive castles, the first a posh hotel (43/HOTELS OUTSIDE TOWN) and the other an imposing ruin on a ridge o/looking the Tyne. A walk through dramatic Border Country steeped in lore. Path obvious at first in either direction, then peters out, but the castle you're going to is always in view. Nice picnic spots nr Crichton. (455/LOTHIANS)

432
C2

START: From Borthwick: A7 S for 16km, past Gorebridge, left at N Middleton; signed. From Crichton: A68 almost to Pathhead, signed then 3km.

7KM XCIRC XBIKE BUS ST ANDR SQ 1-B-2

THE BEST WOODLAND WALKS

Refer to Lothians map on pages 116–17.

433
xD3

DAWYCK GARDENS, nr STOBO: 10km W of Peebles on B712 Moffat rd. Outstn of the Edin Botanics; a 'recent' acquisition, though tree planting here goes back 300yrs. Sloping grounds around the Scrape burn which trickles into the Tweed. Landscaped woody pathways for meditative walks. Famous for shrubs and blue Himalayan poppies. Mar-Oct 10am-6pm.   ADMN

434
C2

HUMBIE WOODS: 25km SE by A68 t/off at Fala. Follow signs for church. Most open woods (beech) beyond car park, through paddock. The churchyard is as reassuring a place to be buried as you could wish for; if you're set on cremation, come here and think of earth. Deep in the woods with the burn besides; after-hrs the sprites and the spirits must have a hell of a time.

435
D1

SMEATON GARDENS, EAST LINTON: 2km from village on N Berwick rd (signed Smeaton). Up a drive in an old estate is this walled grd going back to the early 19th century. An additional pleasure is the Lake Walk halfway down the drive through a small gate in the woods. A 1km stroll round a secret finger lake in magnificent woodland. Grd hrs 10am-4.30pm, Sun from 11.30am; cl w/ends Jan and Feb.

436
E1

WOODHALL DENE, nr DUNBAR: A1 Dunbar bypass, E to Spott then rd to left, 5km. Small car park in river hollow. Follow river to important ancient woodland site (2km). Can be damp. Few folk.

437
C2

DALKEITH COUNTRY PARK: 15km SE by A68. The wooded policies of Dalkeith House; enter at end of Main St. Surprisingly extensive area so close to town and conurbation. Under these stately deciduous trees, carpets of bluebells, daffs and snowdrops, primroses and wild garlic according to season. Adventure playground for kids, natural playground for the rest of us.

438
C2

VOGRIE COUNTRY PARK, nr GOREBRIDGE: 25km S by A7 then B6372 6km from Gorebridge. Small country park well organized for 'recreational pursuits'. 9-hole golf course, tearoom and country ranger staff. May be busy on Sun, but otherwise a corral of countryside on the v edge of town.

CARDRONA FOREST/GLENTRESS, nr PEEBLES: 40km S to Peebles, 8km E on B7062 and similar distance on A72. Cardrona on same rd as Kailzie Grdn Tearoom (Apr-Oct) isexcellent for tea and cake. Forestry Commission woodlands so mostly regimented firs, but Scots pine and deciduous trees up the burn. Set trails incl mt bikes. Nice in late autumn and winter. Some dark mysterious bits.

439
xD3

THE BEST BEACHES

Refer to Lothians map on pages 116–17.

✠ **SEACLIFF:** The best beach, least crowded/littered; perfect for picnics, beachcombing, dreaming and gazing into rock pools. There is a harbour, still in use, which is also good for swimming. 50km from Edin, Seacliff is off the A198 out of N Berwick, 3km after Tantallon Castle (456/LOTHIANS). At a bend in the rd and a farm (Auldhame) there is an unsigned rd off to the left. 2km on there's a barrier, costing 2 x 50p to get car through. Car park 1km then walk. From A1, take E Linton turn-off, go through Whitekirk towards N Berwick, then same.

440
E1

PORTOBELLO: Edin's town beach, 8km from centre by London Rd. When sunny – chips, lager, bad ice cream. When miserable – soulful dog walkers. Arcades, mini-funfair, long prom. A 'used to be' place. (353/SPORTS FACILITIES)

441
C1

YELLOWCRAIGS: Nearest decent beach (35km). A1 or bypass, then A198 coast rd. Left o/side Dirleton for 2km, park and walk 100m across links to fairly clean strand and sea. Gets busy, but big enough to share. Hardly anyone swims, but you can. Scenic. **GULLANE BENTS,** a sweep of beach, is nearby and reached from village main st. Connects westwards with Aberlady Nature Reserve.

442
D1

WHERE TO TAKE KIDS

443
xA3

✚ ✚ **EDINBURGH ZOO:** 334 9171. Corstorphine Rd. 4km W of Princes St. A large and long-established zoo, where the natural world from the poles to the plains of Africa is ranged around Corstorphine Hill. Enough huge/exotic/ghastly creatures and friendly, amusing ones to fill an overstimulated day. The penguins and the seals do their stuff at set times. More familiar creatures hang out at the 'farm'. Café and shop stocked with environmentally OK toys and souvenirs. Open 7 days 9am-6pm (until dusk in winter). (333/MAIN ATTRACTIONS)   ADMN

444
D3

✚ ✚ **MUSEUM OF CHILDHOOD:** 529 4142. 42 High St. An Aladdin's cave of toys through and for all ages. Full of adults saying, 'I had one of them!' Child-size mannequins in upper gallery can foment an *Avengers*-era spookiness if you're up there alone. Much more fascinating than computer games – allegedly. Mon-Sat 10am-5pm. Cl Sun. (339/OTHER ATTRACTIONS)

445
LOTHIANS
C2

✚ **BUTTERFLY FARM, nr DALKEITH:** 663 4932. On A7, signed Eskbank/Galashiels from ring rd (1km). Part of a big complex which includes a grd centre and the revamped and rather swish **BIRDS OF PREY CENTRE** (flying displays; kids get to handle some of the birds, phone for details on 654 1720). As for the bugs, the butterflies are delightful but 'orrible children will be far more impressed with the scorpions, locusts and other assorted uglies on show. Red-kneed tarantula not for the faint-hearted. 7 days, 10am-5pm.

446
LOTHIANS
B1

✚ **DEEP SEA WORLD, NORTH QUEENSFERRY:** 01383 411411. The massively successful aquarium in a quarry which must make life hell in N Queensferry at the w/end (park 'n' ride system and buses from Edin, or better still by *Maid of the Forth* from S Queensferry. Habitats are viewed from a conveyor belt where you can stare goggle-eyed at the goggle-eyed fish teeming around and above you. Poor old Moby the whale's skull is now displayed (he got into trouble in the Forth in 1997) along with Amazonian fish in a 'rainforest habitat'. Maximum hard sell to this all-weather attraction, but kids like it even when they've been queuing for aeons. In my view the best thing is the view from the canteen. Open AYR 7 days: summer 10am-6.30pm; winter 11am-5pm.   ADMN

447

CHILDREN'S FESTIVAL: 554 6297 for info. Annual event held sometime in May somewhere in the capital, possibly in tents. Yes, there were changes afoot when the book was being written but the kids' fest, a week of shows from around the world, is always good fun.

BEST PLACES IN THE LOTHIANS

Refer to Lothians map on pages 116–17.

HISTORICAL PLACES

✝ ✝ ✝ **LINLITHGOW PALACE:** Impressive from the M9 and the S app to this, the most agreeable of W Lothian towns, but don't confuse the magnificent Renaissance edifice with St Michael's Church next door, topped with its controversial crown and spear spire. From the richly carved fountain in the courtyard, to the Gr Hall with its adj huge kitchens, you get a real impression of the lavish lifestyle of the court. Apparently 'under-performs' as an attraction for Historic Scotland, so some titivation may be underway.   HS

448
B1

✝ ✝ **ROSSLYN CHAPEL:** 12 km S of Edin city centre. Take A702, then A703 from ring-route rd, marked Penicuik. Roslin village 1km from main rd and chapel 500m from village crossrds above Roslin Glen (429/WALKS OUTSIDE THE CITY). Freemason central: stories abound of the Holy Grail hidden in the walls and for the next few yrs there's a metal hood to protect the roof. For such a wee chapel visitors can spend hrs wandering around working out the place, with help from copious guidance notes. Founded by a 15th-century Sinclair, Prince of Orkney, who reinterred his 13th-century ancestor here (the latter just happened to be a Grand Prior of the Knights Templar). All holy meaningful stuff in a *Foucault's Pendulum* sense. But a special place. Episcopalian.

449
C2

CAIRNPAPPLE HILL, nr LINLITHGOW: App from the Beecraigs' rd off W end of Linlithgow main st. Go past the Beecraigs t/off and continue for 3km. Cairnpapple is signed. Cairn and remnants of various rings of stones evince the long sequence of ceremonial activities that took place on this high, windy hill betw 2800 and 500 BC. Atmos made even more strange by the very 20th-century communications mast next door. Go into the tomb.   HS

450
A1

CRICHTON CASTLE, nr PATHHEAD: 6km W of A68 at Pathhead (28km S of Edin) or via A7 turning E 3km S of Gorebridge. Massive Border keep dominating the Tyne valley on knoll with church ruin nearby. Spectacular 'range' built late 16th century. 500m walk from Crichton village. Good picnic spot. (432/WALKS OUTSIDE THE CITY)   HS

451
C2

TANTALLON CASTLE, NORTH BERWICK: 5km E of town by coast rd; 500m to dramatic clifftop setting with views to Bass Rock. Dates

452
D1

from 1350 with massive 'curtain wall' to see it through stormy weather and stormy history. The Red Douglases and their friends kept the world at bay. Gr beach nearby (440/BEACHES).

453
D1

HOPETOUN MONUMENT, ATHELSTANEFORD, nr HADDINGTON: The needle atop a rare rise in E Lothian and a gr vantage point from which to view the county from the Forth to the Lammermuirs and Edin over there. Off A6737 Haddington to Aberlady rd on B1343 to Athelstaneford. Car park and short climb. Tower usually open and viewfinder boards at the top. Good gentle 'ridge' walk E from here.

454
D1

GOSFORD HOUSE, nr ABERLADY: On A198 betw Longniddry and Aberlady, the Gosford estate is behind a high wall and strangely stunted vegetation. Imposing house with centre block by Robert Adam and the wing you visit by William Young. The Marble Hall houses the remarkable collections of the unbroken line of the Earls of Wemyss. Botticellis, Rubens and Canalettos and important portraits in delightful informal displays (handwritten cards). No tearoom or paraphernalia here, but the grounds with their ornamental ponds and their Hansel and Gretel curling and ice houses are superb picnic spots. Only open Wed/Sat/Sun 2-5pm, Jun and Jul.

455
D1

THE LAMP OF THE LOTHIANS, ST MARY'S COLLEGIATE, HADDINGTON: Follow signs from E main st. At the risk of sounding profane or at least trite, this is a church that's really got its act together, both now and throughout ecclesiastical history. It's beautiful and in a fine setting on the R Tyne, with good stained glass and interesting crypts and corners. But it's obviously v much at the centre of the community, a lamp as it were, in the Lothians. Guided tours, brass rubbings (Sat), summer recitals (Sun afternoon). Coffee shop and gift shop. Don't miss Lady Kitty's grd nearby, incl the secret medicinal grd, a quiet spot to contemplate (if not sort out) your condition. Apr-Sep Mon-Sat 10am-4pm.

456
D1

THE EAST LOTHIAN CHURCHES AT ABERLADY, WHITEKIRK AND ATHELSTANEFORD: 3 charming churches in bucolic settings; quiet corners to explore and reflect. Easy to find. All have interesting local histories and in the case of Athelstaneford, a national resonance – a 'vision' in the sky nr here became the flag of Scotland, the saltire. An innovative audiovisual display explains. Aberlady my favourite.

OUTDOOR PLACES *Also see* WALKS OUTSIDE THE CITY.

✝ ✝ **ST ABB'S HEAD, nr NORTH BERWICK:** Outwith Lothians, 22 km from N Berwick, 9km N of Eyemouth but only 10km E of main A1. Spectacular cliff scenery, a huge seabird colony, rich marine life and a varied flora make this a place of fascination and diverse interest. Good view from top of stacks, geos and cliff face full of serried ranks of guillemot, kittiwake, razorbill, etc. Hanging grds of grasses and campion. Behind cliffs, grassland rolls down to the Mire L and its varied habitat of bird, insect and butterfly life and vegetation. Superb.

457
xE1

✝ **THE LAGOON, MUSSELBURGH:** On E end of town behind the racecourse (follow rd round), at the estuarine mouth of the R Esk. Waders, seabirds, ducks aplenty and often interesting migrants on the mudflats and wide littoral. The 'lagoon' itself is a man-made pond behind and attracts big populations (both birds and binocs). This is the nearest diverse-species area to Edin (15km) and in recent yrs has become one of the most significant migrant stopovers in the UK.

458
C1

THE LAMMERMUIRS: The hills SE of Edin that divide the rich farm-lands of E Lothian and the valley of the Tweed in the Borders. Mostly a high wide moorland but there's wooded gentle hill coun-try in the watersheds of the southern rivers and spectacular coastal scenery betw Cockburnspath and St Abb's Head. The eastern part of the Southern Upland Way follows the Lammermuirs to the coast. Many moorland walks begin at the car park at the head of Whiteadder Reservoir (A1 to Haddington, B6369 towards Humbie, then E on B6355 through Gifford), a mysterious loch in the bowl of the hills. Excellent walks also centre on Abbey St Bathans to the S. Head off the A1 at Cockburnspath. Through vil-lage to 'Toot' Corner (signed 1km) and off to left, follow path above valley of Whiteadder to Edinshall Broch (2km). Further on, along river (1km), is a swing br and a fine place to swim. Circular walk possible; ask in village.   5-15KM SOME CIRC MTBIKE 1/2-B-2

459
E2

JOHN MUIR COUNTRY PARK, nr DUNBAR: Named after the 19th-century conservationist who founded America's National Parks (and the Sierra Club) and who was born in Dunbar. This swathe of coastline to the W of the town (known locally as Tyninghame) is

460
E1

an important estuarine nature reserve but is good for family walks and beachcombing. Can enter via B6370 off A198 to N Berwick or by 'clifftop' trail from Dunbar.

461
A1

MUIRAVONSIDE COUNTRY PARK: 5km W of Linlithgow on B825. Also signposted from jnct 4 of the M9 Edin/Stirling. Former farm estate now run by the local authority providing 170 acres of woodland walks, parkland, picnic sites and a visitor centre for school parties or anyone else with an interest in birds, bees and badgers. Ranger service does guided walks Apr-Sep. Gr place to walk off that lunch at the none-too-distant Champany's (166/BURGERS).

462
D1

THE BASS ROCK, off NORTH BERWICK: 'Temple of gannets'. A gr guano-encrusted spaceship takeoff ramp sticking out of the Forth and where Davie Balfour was imprisoned in RLS's *Catriona* (aka *Kidnapped* 2). Weather-dependent boat trips available May-Sep courtesy of Mr Marr from N Berwick harbour (also to nearby Fidra). Phone 01620 892838 for details.

ACTIVITY PLACES *Also see* SPORTS FACILITIES.

463
B1

⚓ **LINLITHGOW POOL:** 01506 652783. On edge of pleasant town off rd to Lanark. Modern light and airy sports centre with sauna and steam room at the poolside and W Lothian o/side the windows. Excellent community facility, well designed and laid out. All towns should enjoy this quality of life. This pool is where I go.

464
B1

⚓ **PORT EDGAR, SOUTH QUEENSFERRY:** 331 3330. At end of village, under and beyond the Forth Rd Br. Major marina and watersports centre. Berth your boat, hire anthing from a Wayfarer to a canoe or just use the jetty to kick off some windsurfing or jet-skiing. Big tuition programme for kids. Easter-Oct..

465
E1

DUNBAR POOL: 01368 865456. Model of its kind, o/looking old harbour (where folks used to swim on a summer's day) and castle ruins. Cool, modern design amid the warm red sandstone. Flumes and wave machine that mimics the sea o/side; lengths just possible in betw (though it's often v crowded). 7 days until 8pm (6pm at w/ends).

OTHER MUSTS

466
C1

⚓ ⚓ **LUCA'S, MUSSELBURGH:** 32 High St. Queues in the middle of a Sun afternoon in Feb are testament to the enduring popularity of this legendary ice-cream boutique. 3 classic flavours (vanilla, choc and strawberry) and pure ingredients attract folk from Edin (14km), though there is a branch in the nearby suburb of Craigmillar. Café through the back has basic snacks and ice cream in its sundae best, but you might have to wait when it gets busy. Mon-Sat 9am-10pm, Sun 10.30am-10pm.

✠ ✠ MUSEUM OF FLIGHT, nr HADDINGTON: 01620 880308. 3km from A1 NE of town. In the old complex of hangars and nissen huts at the side of E Fortune, an airfield dating to World War I, a large collection of planes from gliders to jets and esp wartime memorabilia respectfully restored and preserved. Inspired and inspiring displays; not just boys' stuff. Marvel at the bravery back then and sense the unremitting passage of time. From E Fortune the airship R34 made its historic Atlantic crossings. Apr-Oct 7 days; 10.30am-5pm (until 6pm Jul and Aug).

467
D1

GLENKINCHIE DISTILLERY (TOUR), PENCAITLAND: 01875 342004. Only 25km from the city centre (via A68 and A6093 before Pathhead), so popular. Founded in 1837 in a peaceful, pastoral place (it's 3km from the village) with its own bowling green; a country trip as well as a whisky tour. They have occasional 'silent seasons', so check since all you'd see then is a video. New state-of-the art visitor centre opened Dec 1996. May-Sep tours daily until 4pm, Oct-Mar Mon-Fri until 4pm.

468
D2

ROOM AT THE TOP, BATHGATE: 01506 635707. Menzies Rd. You can spend half an hr driving around the centre of Bathgate before you twig that the huge thing next to Safeway is a purpose-built night-club – the UK's biggest. (Cream and Ministry of Sound come on down!) Proprietor doesn't like the word superclub, hyperbole wouldn't do it justice. Opened May 1997, capacity of 2600, more dance floors, bars, nooks and (snogging) crannies than you can count.

469
A2

SAM BURN'S YARD, PRESTONPANS: 01875 810600. On the coast rd out of Musselburgh; if you get to Prestonpans you've missed it. By a gate in the wall you'll see cars on the kerb on a long straight stretch. The yard has piles of old bikes, assorted 'stuff' and is full of domestic and office furniture stored both outdoors and in sheds. Popular with Sun browsers, although you wonder who might want a rusted filing cabinet or a second-hand toilet. 7 days until 5pm, Sun from 12.30pm.

470
C1

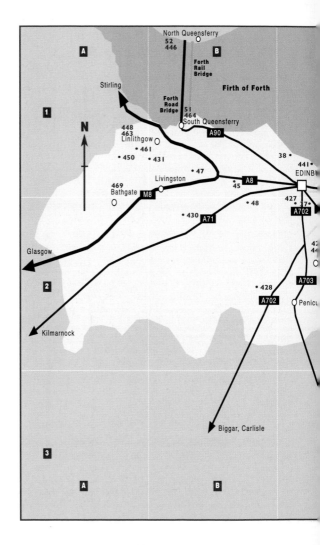

North Queensferry
52
446

Forth
Rail
Bridge

Firth of Forth

Forth
Road
Bridge
51
464
South Queensferry

A90

Stirling

38 •

441•

EDINB

448
463
Linlithgow
• 461
• 450   • 431

• 47

A8

45

469
Bathgate   M8

Livingston

• 48

427
•   7•
A702

• 430   A71

42
44

A703

• 428
A702   Penicu

Glasgow

Kilmarnock

Biggar, Carlisle

116

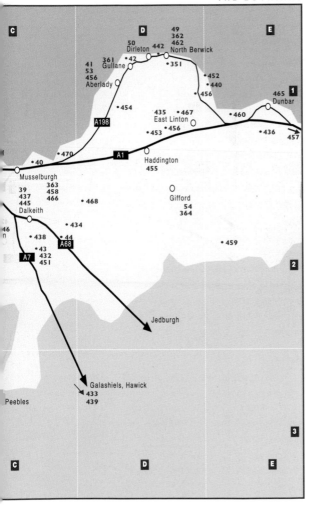

C

D

E

49
362
462
North Berwick

50
Dirleton 442

• 42

361
Gullane

41
53
456
Aberlady

• 351

• 452
• 440

• 456

465
Dunbar

1

• 454

A198

435 • 467
East Linton

• 460

• 453 • 456

• 436
457

• 470

A1

Haddington
455

Musselburgh

39   363
437   458
445   466
Dalkeith

• 468

Gifford
54
364

• 459

• 434

• 438

• 44
A68

• 43
432
451

A7

Jedburgh

Galashiels, Hawick
433
439

Peebles

2

3

C

D

E

SHOPPING GAZETTEER

These are the shops that get it right. SOUTH means S of a central area bisected by Princes St; east is E of the city centre, etc.

ESSENTIALS

Bakers

Bread: **JENNER'S,** see Dept Stores. Only Edin stockist of Fisher & Donaldson's Dr Floyd's bread.

Bread/Italian: **VALVONA & CROLLA,** 19 Elm Row. 556 6066. EAST

Bread: **AULD ALLIANCE,** 32 Victoria St. 622 7080. SOUTH

Pâtisserie: **FLORENTIN,** 8 St Giles St. 225 6267. CENTRAL

Custard pies: **IRVINE'S,** 16 Clerk St. 667 0262. SOUTH

Italian: **FRANCHINO'S PASTICCERIA,** 14 Albert St. 554 7417. EAST

Italian: **ANGELO'S,** 20a Brougham Pl. SOUTH

Barbers

WOODS, 12 Drummond St. 556 6716 SOUTH.

Butchers

Free range: **GEORGE BOWER,** 75 Raeburn Pl. 332 3469. NORTH

Delicatessen

GLASS & THOMPSON, 2 Dundas St. 557 0909. CENTRAL

VALVONA & CROLLA, 19 Elm Row. 556 6066. EAST

PECKHAM'S, 159 Bruntsfield Pl. 229 7054. SOUTH. Also Waverley Stn. CENTRAL

BENNTTTI'S, 9 Randolf Pl. 225 6252. CENTRAL

Mexican: **LUPE PINTO'S,** 24 Leven St. Bruntsfield. 228 6241. SOUTH

Cheese: **IAIN MELLIS,** 30a Victoria St. 226 6215. CENTRAL & 205 Bruntsfield Pl. 447 7414. SOUTH

Cheese: **HERBIE,** 66 Raeburn Pl. 332 9888. NORTH

Department Stores

JENNER'S, Princes St. 225 2442. CENTRAL

General: **JOHN LEWIS,** St James Centre. 556 9121. CENTRAL

Ironmongers

GRAYS, 89 George St. 225 7381. CENTRAL

Fishmongers

GEORGE ARMSTRONG, 80 Raeburn Pl. 315 2033. NORTH. Also at The Gyle Shopping Centre, way out WEST.

CLARK BROS, 2 Harbour New St, Musselburgh. 665 6181. EAST

LONGA FISH, 23 Leven St, Tollcross. 229 2160. SOUTH

SOMETHING FISHY, 16a Broughton St. 556 7614. NORTH

Seafood: **TSE'S FISH MARKET,** 2 Warrender Park Rd. 229 4207. SOUTH

Flowers

RAEBURN GROCERS, 23 Comely Bank Rd. 332 5166. NORTH

GRANTS THE FLORIST, 116 Nicolson St. 668 2660. SOUTH

FLOWERS BY MAXWELL, 32 Castle St. 226 2866. NORTH

Fruit & Veg

FARMER JACK'S, 5 Graham St. 553 6090. EAST

VALVONA & CROLLA, 19 Elm Row. 556 6066. Fresh from Milan. EAST

ARGYLE PLACE: Several shops for fresh produce in this st. SOUTH

Organic: **REAL FOODS,** 37 Broughton St. 557 1911. CENTRAL

Haggis

MACSWEENS, 118 Bruntsfield Pl. 229 9141. SOUTH. Also:

MACSWEENS FACTORY, Dryden Rd, Bilston Glen, Loanhead. 440 2555. 10km S of city.

Hairdressers

CHEYNES, various branches. 225 2234. CENTRAL

CHARLIE MILLER, 13 Stafford St. 226 5550. CENTRAL

Late-night

General: Some 24hr general stores have opened in the last yr – main chains are **ALLDAYS** (Nicolson St, Raeburn Pl) and **COSTCUTTER** (Lothian Rd and elsewhere).

SAINSBURY'S SUPERMARKET, Blackhall. 332 0704. Open 24hrs on Fri night. NORTH

Late Chemists: **BOOTS,** 48 Shandwick Pl. 225 6757. Until 9pm. CENTRAL

Men's Clothes

New labels: **CRUISE,** St Mary's St and 94 George St. 226 3524/556 2532. CENTRAL. Giorgio, Hugo, Ralph, Hughie

SMITHS, 124 High St. 225 5927. CENTRAL

Established labels: **AUSTIN REED,** 39 George St. 225 6703. CENTRAL

Both: **JENNER'S,** Princes St. 225 2442. CENTRAL

HOUSE OF FRASER, 145 Princes St. 225 2472. CENTRAL

Newspapers

INTERNATIONAL NEWSAGENTS, 367 High St. 225 4827. CENTRAL

Oriental Grocers

PAT'S CHUNG YING CHINESE SUPERMARKET, 199 Leith Walk. 554 0358. EAST

SIN FUNG, 16 Bruntsfield Pl. 228 6007. SOUTH

Pasta

GOURMET PASTA, 52 Morningside Rd. 447 4750. SOUTH.

Shoes

Shoes that last: **BARNETS,** 7 High St. 556 3577. CENTRAL.

Modish: **SCHUH,** 32 N Bridge. 225 6552 and 6 Frederick St. 220 0290. Both CENTRAL

Tobacco

THE PIPE SHOP, 92 Leith Walk. 553 3561. EAST

Wholefoods

REAL FOODS, 37 Broughton St. 557 1911. CENTRAL; 8 Brougham St. 228 1201. SOUTH

ROOTS, 60 Newington Rd. 668 2888. SOUTH

Wine & Beer

J. E. HOGG, 61 Cumberland St. 556 4025. NORTH

IRVINE ROBERTSON WINES, 10 N Leith Sands. 553 3521. EAST

PETER GREEN, 37a/b Warrender Park Rd. 229 5925. SOUTH

OASTS & TOASTS, 107-109 Morrison St. 228 8088. WEST

Women's Clothes

New labels: **CORNICHE,** 2 Jeffrey St. 556 3707. CENTRAL

JANE DAVIDSON, 152 Thistle St. 225 3280. CENTRAL

Second-hand: **HAND IN HAND,** 3 NW Circus Pl. 226 3598. NORTH

Hire a posh frock: **DRESS HIRE STUDIO,** 19 Grassmarket. 225 7391.
   CENTRAL

THE MOST INTERESTING SHOPS

Antiques

General: Grassmarket, Victoria St, Thistle St, St Stephen St, NW
   Circus Pl.

Bric-a-brac: **BYZANTIUM,** 9 Victoria St. 225 1768. CENTRAL

UNICORN, 65 Dundas St. 556 7176. NORTH

Jewellery: **JOSEPH BONNAR,** 72 Thistle St. 226 2811. CENTRAL

Clothes: **HAND IN HAND,** 3 NW Circus Pl. 226 3598. NORTH

Bedding

AND SO TO BED, 22 Howe St. 225 6998. NORTH

Brushes

ROBERT CHESSER, 40 Victoria St. CENTRAL

Cards

General: **PAPER TIGER,** Stafford St. 226 5812. 53 Lothian Rd. CEN-
   TRAL

Funniest: **PJ's,** 60 Broughton St. NORTH

Playing/Tarot: **SOMERVILLES,** 82 Canongate. 556 5225. CENTRAL

Ceramics

WARE ON EARTH, 15 Howe St. 558 1276. NORTH

AZTECA, 5 Grassmarket. 229 9368. 16 Victoria St. CENTRAL

Clothes

General: See Shopping For Essentials

Old: **PADDIE BARRASS,** 15 Grassmarket. 226 3087. CENTRAL

ELAINE'S, 53 St Stephen St. NORTH

FLIP, 60 S Br. 556 4966. SOUTH

Outdoor: **GRAHAM TISO,** 13 Wellington Pl. 554 0804. Rose St. EAST

Comics

DEAD HEAD COMICS, 27 Candlemaker Row. 226 2774. CENTRAL

FORBIDDEN PLANET, 3 Teviot Pl. 225 8613. CENTRAL

Cookbooks

CLARISSA DICKSON-WRIGHT'S COOK BOOKSHOP, Grassmarket. 226 4445. CENTRAL

Furniture

Modern: **INHOUSE,** 28 Howe St. 225 2888. NORTH

Traditional: **SHAPES,** 33 W Mill Rd. 441 7963. SOUTH

American: **THE GREAT AMERICAN INDOORS,** 10 Springvalley Gardens. 447 5795. SOUTH

Ice Cream

LUCA'S, 34 High St. Musselburgh. 665 2237. EAST 20km

Jokes

AHA HA HA, 99 West Bow. 220 5252. CENTRAL

Junk

EASY, Couper St, Leith. 554 7077. EAST

JUST JUNK, Broughton St. NORTH

SAM BURNS' YARD, Main rd to Prestonpans. EAST 25km

UTILITIES Broughton St. CENTRAL

Luggage and Bags

A.D. MACKENZIE, 34 Victoria St. 220 0089. CENTRAL

Models

MARIONVILLE MODELS, 42 Turnhouse Rd. 317 7010. WEST

MAC'S MODELS, 168 Canongate. 557 5551. EAST

WONDERLAND, 397 Lothian Rd. 229 6428. CENTRAL

Presents

ROUND THE WORLD, 82 W Bow and NW Circus Pl. 225 7086. CENTRAL/NORTH

OUT OF THE NOMAD'S TENT, St Leonard's Lane. 662 1612. SOUTH

STUDIO ONE, 10 Stafford St. 226 5812.

BLACKADDER GALLERY, 5 Raeburn Pl. 332 4605. NORTH

GALERIE MIRAGES, 46a Raeburn Pl. 315 2603. NORTH

Rude Stuff

LEATHER & LACE, 8 Drummond St. 557 9413. SOUTH

WHIPLASH TRASH, 53 Cockburn St. 226 1005. SOUTH

Rugs

ORIENTAL RUGS OF DISTINCTION, 297 Canongate. 556 6952. CENTRAL

WHYTOCK AND REID, Belford Mews. 226 4911. WEST

Sci-fi

FORBIDDEN PLANET, 3 Teviot Pl. SOUTH

Souvenirs

See below and **ANYWHERE ON THE HIGH ST.**

Tartan, serious: **KINLOCH ANDERSON,** Commercial St. 555 1355. EAST

HECTOR RUSSELL, Princes St/High St. CENTRAL

Tartan and tacky: Not hard to find.

Sports

MACKENZIE'S, 17 Nicolson St. 667 2288. SOUTH

MOMENTUM, 22 Bruntsfield Pl. 229 6665. SOUTH (SURFING)

WHITE STUFF, Hanover St. 624 2424. NORTH (SNOWBOARDING)

AITKEN AND NIVEN, 77-79 George St. 225 1461. CENTRAL

Sweets

CASEY JAMES, 52 St Mary's St. SOUTH

Tiles

THE ORIGINAL TILE CO, 23a Howe St. 556 2013. NORTH

Video Rental

ALPHABET VIDEO, 22 Marchmont Rd. 229 5136. SOUTH

C & A VIDEO, 93 Broughton St. 556 1866. CENTRAL

Woollies

JUDITH GLUE, 64 High St. 556 5443. CENTRAL

NUMBER TWO, St Stephen Pl. 225 6257. NORTH

BILL BABER, 66 Grassmarket. 225 3249. CENTRAL

THE CASHMERE STORE, 2 St Giles St. 225 4055. CENTRAL

HILLARY ROHDE, 332 4147 (exclusive cashmere; by appointment only)

BORTHWICK CASTLE 'this magnificent tower house knocks you off your horse with its authenticity' (page 25)

INDEX

Index

COLLINS

Other titles by Peter Irvine published by HarperCollins*Publishers* are:

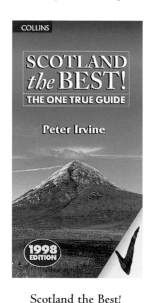

Glasgow the Best!

ISBN 0 00 472153 5

£5.99

Scotland the Best!

ISBN 0 00 472150 0 (hardback)

£12.99

ISBN 0 00 472151 9 (paperback)

£9.99